ISBN: 978129018105

Published by:
HardPress Publishing
8345 NW 66TH ST #2561
MIAMI FL 33166-2626

Email: info@hardpress.net
Web: http://www.hardpress.net

WHITE MAGIC

MR. JASPER MASKELYNE WITH HIS WIFE AND FAMILY

WHITE MAGIC

The Story of Maskelynes

By

JASPER MASKELYNE

Treasure Library

LONDON

STANLEY PAUL & CO., LTD.

PRINTED IN
GREAT BRITAIN,
AT THE ANCHOR
PRESS, TIPTREE,
:: ESSEX ::

CONTENTS

CONTENTS

WHITE MAGIC

CHAPTER I

What is magic?—The Black Arts and the White—A farming family goes to the Devil!—Did Nevil Maskelyne practise witchcraft?—The Maskelyne tradition—"J. N." becomes a watchmaker—Friendship with Cooke—Attending spiritualistic séances—Advent of the Davenports.

THERE are a number of answers to the question "What is magic?". Doubtless some of my readers who have played faro or highball poker with strangers can give one definition. Victims of the three-card trick or the manipulated dice have their own ideas. People who, in these enlightened times, still openly believe in ghosts, spirit manifestations, and wart-charming, can explain yet another form of magic, though they cannot explain it away.

For myself, I believe in only one sort of mystification, and that is White Magic. I grant a respectful reservation towards the Black Arts, not because I can practise them myself, but as the result of some rather eerie experiences which I shall detail later.

In the main, however, this book, being a history of the Magic House of Maskelyne, deals with the gentle art of illusion only, and the adventures that have befallen three generations of us who have made a living by deluding the public.

Other wizards—the share-pushers and gold-brick sellers of our times—have perhaps been even more financially successful, and had more exciting lives. But I claim that we Maskelynes, from my grandfather, "J. N.", to myself,

the youngest of his grandchildren, have won greater amusement and more happiness than even these "big shots" of
this world of illusion.

Yet, curiously enough, our family connection with
magic had a black beginning, if legend speaks true. For
there is an ancient story, laughed at as such tales are bound
to be by each succeeding generation of Maskelynes (though
one apologetically touches wood or crosses one's fingers
at the time), to the general effect that a certain farmer of our
name once sold himself, with entail rights over the next
ten generations of us, to the Devil. From that day, so the
chronicle runs, we have all been possessed of magic powers.

John Maskelyne, burly sixteenth-century farmer, respected
squire, and Justice of the Peace, was called to pass sentence
one day on a little twisted black man, in a black silk suit,
known only by the queer appellation of the Drummer of
Tedworth. The little person was most clearly proved guilty
of witchcraft, and was sent to the plantations.

A month after he had left these shores in the prison-ship
queer rumours began to get abroad concerning Farmer
Maskelyne. A little black man was seen limping about his
farm. He himself, morose and fearful, hardly ever stirred
from the sprawling farmhouse under the wood.

His red cattle died of a murrain. A fire driven by a strange
wind burned down his corn-ricks after harvest, and a little
black figure was seen dancing in the flames. The farmer
began to gamble, and lost more money than he possessed.

And then his prosperity returned with unnatural
rapidity. The empty Wiltshire fields were suddenly stocked
with twice as many cattle as he had formerly owned. One
morning in February, during a local famine, he said that his
barns were bursting with corn—the corn that had been
burned six months earlier. His pockets clinked with gold.

Then he died—or some said he disappeared one night,

flying on great black wings athwart racing storm-clouds, while the figure of the little twisted man gambolled about him.

So much for the legend. According to its sequel, John Maskelyne had bought, by the sale of his soul, Black Magic powers not only for himself but for ten generations of his descendants.

Although we modern representatives of the family take the tale lightly, the ranks of the credulous seem hardly thinned since good King Charles's golden reign. For Maskelynes ever since have been accused of dark and dirty dealings with the Little Black Man.

Nevil Maskelyne, Royal Astronomer to King George III, found his early career seriously hampered by gossip-mongers who persistently spread the libel that his know-ledge of the stars in their courses sprang from the prompt-ings of a black-coated familiar who was as conversant with the star-ways as Nevil himself was with the byways of old Westminster.

Throughout all the latter part of his career, it is true that this Nevil had only one assistant. Between them they originated the now world-famous *Nautical Almanack* following a voyage on which Nevil had determined the transit of Venus and other astral calculations.

He invented the prismatic micrometer, measured time to tenths of a second, ascertained the weight of the earth, and taught us much of what we know about latitude and longitude. And, following each of his new discoveries, there came the murmur of those who remembered the old legends concerning John Maskelyne's dealings with a limp-ing gentleman in black to whom all these things were mere nursery knowledge.

The astronomer's one assistant was sometimes said to be the Little Gentleman in Black !

A lady ancestress of mine who seems to have escaped entirely the evil effects of the Devil legend, though there were those who attributed her amazing marriage to supernatural agencies, was Margaret Maskelyne, sister of the astronomer and wife of Clive of India.

Lord Clive fell in love with her before he saw her— and if that isn't magic, what is? The stern martinet and powerful ruler of India went one day into the apartments of a brother officer, Captain Maskelyne, and saw hanging there a miniature of a lovely dark girl with downcast eyes and a merry, roguish mouth.

The General went over to the portrait and studied it attentively before asking whom it represented. The Captain replied that it was his little sister Margaret, most divine and bewitching of females, and—a spinster.

Then and there, Lord Clive expressed a desire to marry her. Love at first sight, magic—call it what you will, but it is true.

A formal offer of his hand followed; dark Margaret studied the portrait of the famous soldier submitted for her approval; and a few weeks later she was on her way in a full-rigged ship to India, since public opinion at home was then dangerously high against Clive, and he deemed it more prudent not to leave his adopted land. In 1753 they were married at Madras, and Macaulay tells us that they were devoted to each other and lived happily ever after.

Another West-Country Maskelyne of the same line was born in 1839. Astronomy had by this time been given up for the greater attractions of the old farm under the wood, whence the original naughty John was said to have flown on his great black wings two hundred years before. It is my greatest ambition in life to return when I retire to that grey Cotswold farm, with its dry-stone walls and stone-tiled roof; I am even prepared to risk meeting the Little Black

Man there, when I could perhaps show him some tricks too modern yet to have reached his own repertoire.

Before I commence the more authentic history of the modern House of Maskelyne with the story of my grand-father, John Nevil, born in 1839, I must say a brief word about the Devil legend as it has impinged on his life, and my father's, and my own.

"J. N." was constantly accused, often by people who should have had more intelligence, of having the power to expose spiritualist and similar trickery, as demonstrated by the Davenports and others, simply because he was in league with the Father of Tricks.

The same accusation, the Gospels tell us, was levelled against a certain Divine Teacher nearly twenty centuries ago, and His answer has sufficed for all time—that a house divided against itself cannot stand, and how therefore can devils be cast out by the Prince of Devils?

In my own experience, I have received endless letters, many of them scurrilous and offensive in the extreme, accusing me of obtaining my stage effects by the aid of the Black Arts, telling me that I must be in league with the Evil One, and—in different vein, though still apparently intended seriously—telling me that I am the head of a magic London crime gang.

Sometimes, as I read these often ill-spelt epistles, I cannot resist a little sigh of envy. What an illusionist I should be if I were as great as these unconscious syco-phants claim for me!

To return to my grandfather, the founder of Maskelyne and Cooke's, and to my mind incomparably the greatest magician of modern or any other times—with the possible exception of Moses. Unlike myself, he did not take kindly to a farming atmosphere, showing a very early aptitude for mechanics which was later to make his fame and fortune.

For his tricks were almost all of them beautiful demonstrations of applied mechanics.

It is said that he began his career by taking to pieces a wonderful "turnip" watch belonging to his father. That stern parent immediately vowed, with a certain grim humour, considering the mess his beloved watch was probably in at the time, that J. N. should be apprenticed to a Cheltenham watchmaker, and learn how to correct the harm he had so innocently done.

And so J. N., a budding dandy of the leisurely Early Victorian era, no doubt longing for the time when he could sport Dundrearies like his master, was bound apprentice to the watchmaking profession, and first really takes the stage, as far as this history is concerned, swinging his cane and swaggering along the Cheltenham sidewalks, no doubt rolling most devastating eyes at the crinolined damsels who minced past beside stately Mammas while he strode on his predestined way towards the street-corner where he was to collide with another young West-Countryman of the name of Cooke.

I have often heard my grandfather talk of that accidental meeting. They seem to have stared at each other and begun the formal and high-flown apologies of the age—and then, simultaneously, broken down in most unconventional laughter. They shook hands, exchanged names—and so began a partnership whose fame was later to spread into the four corners of the earth.

The friendship so strangely started seems to have developed spasmodically for some time. Both lads were idly interested in conjuring, and this passed from an amusement for leisure moments into a real hobby. With J. N. it commenced the grand passion of his life.

In company with half a dozen acquaintances in Cheltenham, these two young men started a sort of conjuring club.

They used to meet at the house of one or other of the members, give demonstrations of their latest acquirements in the way of tricks, study books whose subjects ranged from witchcraft to legerdemain, and develop simple mechanisms that helped to provide various startling illusions.

J. N. took the lead among them from the first. He had the personality of a Barnum or a C. B. Cochran, and was even then a born showman with a true sense of dramatic possibilities. Moreover, his work as a watchmaker enabled him to attain a surprising proficiency over delicate and minute machinery, some of which could easily be adapted to the purposes of magic.

My grandfather's interest in mechanical illusions was aroused when he was a boy of twelve, when he saw at a London exhibition a wonderful "piping bullfinch". I have heard him say in his later years that, above all his own extraordinary inventions, he set this forgotten marvel of 1851, and that it directly prompted him to commence his experiments with magic mechanisms which began, when he was sixteen, with an elaborate apparatus for optical illusions, and culminated with "Psycho" and its contemporaries.

In 1848, nine years after my grandfather was born, a Mr. and Mrs. Fox and their daughters in New York began what appears to have been the world's biggest hoax, which almost immediately gained the name of spiritualism. When J. N. was a young man, still faithfully doing his duty by the timepieces of Cheltenham, his interest in spiritualism was aroused in a curious way.

Into his shop one day there walked a strange-looking man, with long hair and beard, who gave the young assistant a curious bit of apparatus. He explained at some length that it had a broken spring, and that he wanted the spring renewed, but he deftly turned aside a tentative inquiry as to its purpose.

J. N. mended it satisfactorily, and might have forgotten the incident but for the strange behaviour of the gentleman when he came to pay for the repair. He tested the instrument carefully, waggled his beard, and put down a golden half-sovereign on the counter. The cost of the repair was only a matter of a couple of shillings.

"I'm sure a useful young man like you will know what to do with the change," he said confidentially. "And in return—just forget that you've seen me."

Which, of course, astounded J. N., who got the idea that the visitor was some sort of housebreaker, and that the apparatus was part of his burglar's outfit. So he politely refused the bribe and thought the more.

Two days later, at a meeting of the young Cheltenham magicians—it might have been called the origin of the present-day Magic Circle, that meeting—a member mentioned casually that one of the new-fangled American "spiritualists" was giving a magic-show at Devizes, and that in it invisible hands, said to be those of the dead, rapped on the table, thus answering questions put to them by the bearded old professor who acted as medium.

In a moment J. N. thought of the instrument he had repaired. It was an automatic table-tapper ; a most ingenious little instrument, invisible from the audience, but easily operated by anyone standing near the table.

Before the meeting broke up that night its members had vowed themselves to a campaign of exposure of all fraudulent mediums using mechanical table-tappers. Devizes was a long way from Cheltenham, but there was some hope that the bearded gentleman might come nearer, when the young magicians promised themselves some fun.

However, no séances were held within reasonable distance of the town where the tapper had been repaired ;

doubtless the medium was wise in his generation. The ardour of the young conjurers died down for a while.

And then, superseding the other idea for a time, there came the bright suggestion of giving some amateur entertainments of magic in Cheltenham. I suspect that the lure of the bright eyes that shone so roguishly when their owners curtseyed down into their crinolines may have had something to do with this decision. I like to think of the girls of that day whispering excitedly to one another: "Oh, that *dreadful* Mr. Maskelyne is giving a legerdemain performance on Wednesday evening. I'm going to try *so* hard to get Aunt Louisa to take me. Mr. Cooke will be there, too ; and they are going to do the most *appalling* things !"

At least, Maskelyne and Cooke and their amateur magic circle began to gain some sort of recognition among their townsmen as young fellows who knew a thing or two, and might be pretty well relied upon to detect any trickery that was going.

And so it happened that when the town buzzed with comment, one day, following the display of some chaste little announcements that the Davenport Brothers were coming to Cheltenham, the citizens, burgesses and landgraves went *in posse* to young Messrs. Cooke and Maskelyne and asked them to uphold the burgh's reputation for sharpness by joining the committee that was to watch, at close quarters, the amazing tricks of these said Davenports, and ensure that the spirits with whom they communed were really spirits, and, in fact, that there was nothing up the Davenport sleeve.

Now these Davenports had already gained a very great reputation, not only in England, but abroad as well. Immediately after the world got to hear of the mysterious happenings at the Fox *ménage* in New York, two American brothers, sons of a Buffalo policeman named Davenport, found that they too could hold communication with the spirits of the vasty deep.

Tied hand and foot, as a sop to scoffers who feared that they did it themselves, they called upon furniture to jump about, musical instruments to play, tables to rap and bells to ring ; and, since they were so obviously tied and could not assist—well, it must have been the spirits of the dead who performed these miracles.

Dr. J. B. Ferguson, a Presbyterian minister, joined forces with them, and together the trio toured the United States, gaining great kudos (and fortune), and subsequently came to London, where they gave their first séance, on September 28th, 1864, at the house of Dion Boucicault. The *Morning Post* reported the marvels that ensued in the following words :

At the upper end of the apartment was placed a skeleton wardrobe, fitted with a seat. The doors consisted of three panels, which shut inside with a brass bolt.

The brothers Davenport, having seated themselves *vis-à-vis* on the end bench, their hands and feet were securely tied. . . . A guitar, a tambourine, a violin and bow, a brass horn, and a couple of bells were placed on the seat inside, and the doors shut. . . . Instantly, "hands" were observed through an opening in the wardrobe door. A gentleman present was invited to pass his hand through this opening, and it was "touched" by the "hands" several times.

Musical instruments and bells commenced making all sorts of noises, snatches of airs were distinctly heard, when suddenly the wardrobe door thrust open, the trumpet was thrown out into the room and fell heavily on the carpet. . . .

A moment or two later, the Davenports were found sitting unbound with the ropes at their feet. After an interval of two minutes, the brothers were found to be securely bound with the same cords, the ends being some distance from their hands. . . .

One of the company present was then invited to take a seat in the cabinet. . . . A gentleman having volunteered to be imprisoned, his hands were tied to the knees of the Davenports, whose hands were fastened behind their backs. The instant the door was closed, hands were passed over his face, his hair was gently pulled, and musical instruments lying on his knees were played upon, while a tambourine beat time on his head. . . . Later, several persons in the audience were touched by flying instruments, which on one occasion became so demonstrative that one gentleman received a knock on the nasal organ which broke the skin and caused a few drops of blood to flow. . . .

A Mr. Fay sat in a chair on the stage, and the instant the light was extinguished a whizzing noise was heard. "It's off!" exclaimed Mr. Fay. A candle was lighted, and his coat was found lying in the middle of the room. . . ."

And so on and so on. Someone else's coat was laid on a table, and in a moment of darkness it transferred itself to the shoulders of the coatless Mr. Fay, who, by the way, was an assistant of the Davenports. A gold watch mysteriously fled from the hand of its owner to the feet of Dr. Ferguson.

The audience, after a two hours' séance, were invited to examine the cabinet, the coats, the musical instruments and so on, and professed themselves absolutely satisfied that these things contained no apparatus that could help in obtaining the phenomena. In passing, I should say that reporters, of whom there were many present, must have been simpler in those days than they are now.

Well, of course, after this séance the reputation of the Davenports was made, as far as sleepy old England was concerned. They toured with great honour and profit, after a long London engagement, and in the fullness of time Fate brought them to the Town Hall, in St. James's Square, Cheltenham, where twenty-six-year-old John Nevil Maskelyne was destined to expose their trickery to an astounded world.

J. N. was already enough of a magician himself to have refused utterly to explain away the tricks of a brother in the craft. But these Davenports definitely claimed that they were not illusionists but media, and that not they but the spirits of the dead created the effects which had so impressed the representative of the *Morning Post* and his

B

friends in London. They asked the towns they visited to empanel committees to watch them at close quarters, so as to show that no trickery was used.

.As I have said, my grandfather was among those chosen to act as the eyes of Cheltenham. He was, as he often said to me later, actuated by nothing more than curiosity in accepting the honour. He had an open mind ; he was prepared to be convinced that communication with the dead had really been established. But he was not prepared to countenance any chicanery whose works he himself could expose, more particularly since spiritualism was even then attracting to itself innumerable unhappy people who had lost their loved ones, and who were only too ready to be credulous when the Davenports and their smooth ex-Presbyterian friend offered eloquence and bell-ringings in exchange for expensive tickets of admittance.

The stage is set ; all Cheltenham, from Dundrearies to petticoats, is agog with excitement ; the Great Davenports are here, ready to speak with the departed, and that young Mr. Maskelyne, the amateur conjurer, is to sit on the stage and see fair play.

In my next chapter I will ring up the curtain on that historic Cheltenham stage, and at the same time ring it up on the history of three generations of professional illusionists of whom I am the last.

CHAPTER II

THE afternoon of the Davenport Brothers' performance
at the Cheltenham Town Hall was a fine one, and the
inhabitants of the town flocked through the streets towards
the meeting-hall, anxious to see the very first effort at com-
municating with the dead ever publicly made there.

Doubtless there were wild conjectures flying among the
audience as it packed tighter and tighter into the Town
Hall. Would any local people be recognized by the onlookers when the Davenports recalled them from the
grave ? What messages would the spirits give ? How *could*
a bound man release himself from tight ropes and ring bells,
all in a matter of seconds, and then appear rebound again ?
Would young Mr. Maskelyne detect trickery ? Depend upon
it, he would see it, if any took place.

The hall was filled. The doors were shut. Dark blinds
were drawn across all the windows, while Dr. Ferguson,
a benign and commanding figure, explained from the stage
that the spirits dreaded light and could not communicate
happily save in darkness.

With unctuous solemnity he announced that Ira Erastus
and William Henry Davenport were gifted by Heaven,
and that they worked by spirit-craft alone, not by "the wit-
craft of the commercial". They had, he said in his deep
voice, nothing whatever to do with the ringing of the bells
or other phenomena presently to be witnessed. They

remained bound and motionless all the time ; but, by communing with the spirits of the dead, they enabled the latter to manifest, for the glory of God and the greater enlightenment of weak humanity.

To prove conclusively that no human agency was employed, Dr. Ferguson asked that here, as in London and elsewhere, a chosen quorum of townsmen should come and sit on the platform and if they could detect any fraud or trickery by the Brothers there to declare it.

A small *posse* of frock-coated Cheltenham men advanced on to the platform and seated themselves there. Among them were my grandfather and his friend, young Cooke.

Finally, the Davenports, clad in black, with long dark hair, heavy moustaches and black goatee beards, Ira in his usual attitude with one hand inside his coat and modestly veiling his heart, walked on to the stage amid enormous applause, and sat down.   They were bound hand and foot to their bench, the townsmen assisting in the tying and thoroughly examining all the knots ; the skeleton wardrobe was wheeled on to the stage and examined ; and the musical instruments placed in position.

Then the lights were turned out.   Almost immediately bells began to ring, music was played, hands were seen apparently floating about the wardrobe, and frightened and excited exclamations, some pious and some quite otherwise, were surprised from the packed audience.

As a small boy it was my constant delight to persuade my grandfather to recount to me what followed. As nearly as possible, I will now recall his own words.

"I was sitting at the side of the stage, watching hard, and waiting for the advent of a little surprise I had planned with the aid of another member of our conjuring club. When I judged that the centre of the wardrobe was due to open I tapped with my foot on the floor.

"At that signal, my friend arranged that the blind at one of the windows should be drawn aside a little, admitting a spear of afternoon sunshine just as the wardrobe door opened and instruments began to fly out of it.

"*In the light, I clearly saw Ira Davenport throwing the instruments out of the wardrobe.*

"He cast one startled glance towards the window, jumped back to his bench, wriggled his shoulders with incredible quickness—and as I jumped to my feet to announce the swindle, the lights went up, and there were both brothers, sitting in their places, the ropes that bound them still so tightly tied that they actually cut into the flesh.

"Dr. Ferguson, who had been watching us like a lynx all the time, padded swiftly up to me before I could speak, and whispered urgently to me not to say anything till I had discussed the matter privately with him. I refused.

" 'Ladies and Gentlemen,' I called loudly above the din of clapping and exclamation, 'I have discovered the method by which these tricks are performed.'

"The audience was stricken into silence as if I had shown them the Gorgon's head.

" 'I challenge that statement!' called the lessee of the Town Hall.

" 'I am perfectly prepared to make good my words,' I shouted above the uproar that was gathering. 'The tricks are performed by dexterity and practice. Within three months I guarantee to reproduce every one of these tricks myself, here in this place, and absolutely without any spirit aid whatsoever.' "

Well, of course, my grandfather's statement produced a really first-class sensation. One of the Davenports started an harangue, but was dragged off the stage by his brother and Ferguson. The latter came running back, panting sorely, and tried to shout something about "this misguided young gentleman" and "his preposterous claims".

But the meeting, as a séance attended by the shades, was really pretty well ruined. The audience emerged into the daylight of the Cheltenham streets, buzzing like bees from an overturned hive. Rumour ran hot-foot before them. I should think the local pubs did good business that night, and tittle-tattle probably re-echoed even over the most exclusive of Cheltenham's tea-tables.

As for the Davenports, they had survived attempts at exposure before. They just moved on, in dignified sorrow, going to as many English towns as they could while the going was good.

Less than two months after their historic meeting, Cheltenham was placarded with the first playbill ever produced by Maskelyne and Cooke.

It announced that on Monday evening, June 19th, 1865, these two young gentlemen would give a grand exposition at the Aviary Gardens of the entire public séance of the Davenport Brothers. The performance was scheduled to take place in open daylight, without the aid of spirits, and it offered to duplicate all the Davenport tricks, and to exhibit many others even more astonishing.

It was always a trait in my grandfather's character that he was not content unless he gave his public really good measure!

The Town Hall had been crowded, but the Aviary Gardens were filled to overflowing! Among the audience there were several bewhiskered gentlemen from the London papers, grimly determined not to be duped any more.

A cabinet like the Davenport wardrobe was brought on to the platform first, and was tapped, measured, felt and shaken by everyone present who wished to test it. Two of the reporters, with the aid of a tarry sailor imported for the occasion, tied my grandfather and Cooke inside the cabinet, which was big enough to accommodate them comfortably. The sailor expressed himself briefly and vividly about the strength of the ropes, and he was a critical man.

Immediately the doors of the cabinet were closed, this time in full daylight, they were thrown open again from the inside, and the sailor, running forward with the reporters and some Cheltenham men at his heels, found the two "magicians" as securely tied as ever, in their original places.

The doors were shut again, bells rang, tambourines played wildly, and naked hands appeared in the aperture of the doors, which had opened immediately to admit them. A man ran forward and flung the doors wide, but Messrs. Cooke and Maskelyne still sat bound in their places.

A man from the audience, being critical, was invited to ascend to the platform, where he was blindfolded and seated inside the cabinet. His hands were tied to the knees of the two operators, and the doors were again shut. A Bedlam of music was heard from inside, the doors opened of their own accord, and the blindfolded gentleman was seen still bound as before, with my grandfather and his assistant tied hand and foot beside him, the only change being that a tambourine had perched itself rakishly on the head of the newcomer.

He retired among the audience feeling that his doubts had received a technical knock-out.

The performers then had a few more ropes tied round them by members of the audience who wanted the job done thoroughly ; and, on the suggestion of a cynic, all the knots were sealed with heavy wax seals, bearing the signet imprint of one of the onlookers. Another helpful gentleman suggested that the hands of the magicians should be filled with flour. This was done.

The doors of the cabinet were closed, whereupon two cornets inside instantly began a duet of "Home, Sweet Home!" about the choice of which there seems to have been an impish appropriateness.

As the last chord died away, eager hands plucked the doors of the cabinet wide open, but Messrs. Cooke and Maskelyne still sat, bound, sealed and floured, and quite unflurried. No flour was to be seen on the ropes or spilled in the cabinet.

At this point in the performance the sailor who had acted as professional knotter had to be led outside because he was paying audible tribute in the language the Senior Service felt that the occasion demanded.

After many of the audience had examined the seals, to see that they had not been tampered with, the doors were closed again, while the two performers, still in their sealed ropes and with the flour in their hands, sat silently within.

Four minutes later they both emerged from the cabinet, totally unfettered, and with the flour still unspilled in their hands. The newspaper reports next day said that they were smiling. I can well believe it.

After this they began to get really sensational!

Grandfather announced that he would permit himself to be shut in a heavy deal box, three feet long by two feet wide and eighteen inches deep. The box was duly produced, inspected by a dozen or two of the audience, and passed as free of tricks.

It must have been a bit of a squash to get into it, but he managed it. The box was then locked, and the key tossed among the audience. Another man from the audience then roped up the box so that the woodwork was almost covered, and sealed the ropes. He took seven minutes over this part of the job.

The box was then placed in the big cabinet used for the previous tricks, and a careful gentleman in the audience—it seems to have been composed mainly of such cynical people—suggested the placing of several bells on top of the box. The cabinet doors were closed and bolted.

Immediately the bells began to ring; within a couple of minutes they came flying through the gradually opening doors of the cabinet; and when those doors flew wide at last Grandfather was seen sitting on top of the box, which was found to be still locked, roped and sealed as before.

The man in the audience who still held the key of the box told this one, later in the evening, to the sailor knotting-specialist. I am unable to print his reply, but it was one of the few comments that really did justice to the performance.

And now what had begun as a dare in the interests of truth developed into a theatrical touring company. That night after the Cheltenham show, with the wine of the applause still in their heads, Cooke and my grandfather decided to throw up their steady employment in the town and take their magic on tour.

It was a venturesome decision for two young men to reach in those staid days. Victorians in the main looked on the stage as the Devil's playground. Even in our own more tolerant era fortune is apt to frown on lads who propose, entirely without previous experience, to go into management on their own, without a penny to back them, and with an entirely novel turn to show.

For the young men proposed, by means of amusing interludes, patter and brilliant mechanical illusions, to attempt something quite different from the well-worn conjuring devices current in their day. They set out to revolutionize professional magic. The wonder is that they did it, equipped with nothing else than their own courage, and did it on a scale that has now changed conjuring methods throughout the world.

An epic could have been written about the early adventures of this initial Maskelyne and Cooke tour. At first, great audiences flocked to see the exposers of the Daven-ports. But the thing was a seven-day wonder; without the morbid sensational appeal that the spiritualists themselves monopolized in this connection it soon ceased to attract.

Events moved in a vicious circle. Grandfather could not afford to advertise; he could not afford to give time and money to the invention of mechanical tricks with ideas for which his brain teemed; it soon looked as though an ignominious return to Cheltenham and watchmaking was the only thing left to do.

The manager of a hall in Bold Street, Liverpool, was approached as a last resource, and he agreed, reluctantly enough, to "farm" the show for a month as an experiment. He admitted himself vastly impressed with the entertain-ment, but was uncertain if it would appeal to his public.

It didn't! Perhaps it was too clever. Anyway, at the end of the month the manager declined to back the show any further. Matters became desperate.

It was at this critical juncture that a Mr. William Morton sent in his card one day, and asked to see my grandfather. Mr. Morton, who was only twenty-seven at the time, had already been a journalist, solicitor's clerk, compositor and bookseller, coming badly to grief in his last role, and having to start again, this time as a concert agent.

He saw Maskelyne and Cooke's show, and offered to finance a tour for them through Lancashire, on fifty-fifty terms. It was a godsend to them, and they accepted.

At the end of the first month, no profits had been made at all. But Mr. Morton, who is still alive, and who, at ninety-five, recently began yet another new adventure by

writing his first book, an intensely interesting little auto-
biography, was fearless and confident in his own judgment.
He continued to back the show.

At one period he was actually paying both the performers' minute salaries as well as meeting all expenses.

It was typical of J. N. that he invented a device, when
things were at their worst, which instantly attracted new
attention to the show, and appealed far more to provincial
audiences than any of his duplications of the authentic
Davenport spiritualistic tricks.

The mechanism in this case was a small casket, made
of metal, plain and innocent in appearance, and open to
the most critical examination. In this casket, marked coins,
rings, etc., borrowed from the audience, were placed.
Any member of the onlookers could then bind round the
casket with tape or string, and seal all the knots. If desired,
he could supply his own materials.

J. N. would then take the casket from the hands of the
man who had secured it, and pass it instantly to any other
member of the audience who wished to participate in the
trick. The bonds were unbroken, the seals untouched—
but, in transit, all the articles mysteriously passed from the
closed casket into the possession of the conjurer.

He could produce them from the ears and mouths of
yet other members of the audience, if so desired ; the
marvel was the transference of the articles from the box in
the half-minute or so permitted during the passing of the
casket from hand to hand.

This trick was instantaneously successful. Audiences
began to increase ; instead of always seeking frenziedly
for bookings, Mr. Morton, the new manager of the show,
could sometimes pick among the offers he received ; the
corner was turned and profits at last began to come in.

A year had now gone by from the time when Maskelyne

and Cooke gave their first public performance at Cheltenham. Even now, though engagements were starting to come
in on their own accord, matters were precarious at times.

In the summer of 1866, during a spell of wonderful
weather, audiences shrank almost to zero. The show was
playing in Lancashire, and the receipts at the end of a swel-
tering July week were not nearly enough to cover the rent
due on the Saturday night to the lessees of the hall.

On that Saturday morning, Morton, Cooke, and J. N.
went round the town placarding it with startling red bills.

A FREE GIFT ! !

Maskelyne and Cooke, the famous illusionists and exposers
of so-called Spiritualists, are now performing at the Town Hall.
Tonight, every person paying for admission will be given

HALF A CROWN

Come early to avoid the crush ! !

In case I ever need to try the same one myself, I mean to
preserve the secret of how it was done. But it *was* done, and
done to the entire satisfaction of the hard-headed Lancas-
trian audience.

The hall that night accommodated just under one
thousand paying patrons, and a couple of hundred more
were turned away when it had been packed so that the
doors would hardly shut.

Enormous applause lasted for several minutes after the
curtain had finally rung down. As for the takings, they
paid the expenses for the week and left a margin of profit.

A couple of weeks later the show was in trouble again.
A lady taking part in one of the advertised turns was
suddenly taken ill, and no substitute could be found. Mr.
Morton himself had to act in her stead.

He got into skirts and bustles, and J. N. announced

from the stage that, his assistant having fallen ill, a well-known local lady amateur was helping him in the trick. Mr. Morton then put on his feathered hat, pulled his veil well down to hide his moustache, and tripped on to the stage amid welcoming applause.

Fortunately, he had nothing to say, for he was a little affected with a stammer. But fate tried to interfere in another way. Before he had been on the stage two minutes, J. N. whispered to him in an agitated aside : "Don't turn round, Mr. Morton. Keep your face to the audience. *Something's bust !*"

The scene was cut down as much as possible, but Mr. Morton only just got off the stage in time !

Better business was done in the winter of 1866, but the following summer began to empty the houses once more. J. N. prayed for rain, sleet and thunder, but even he could not produce magic of that calibre.

When things were at their worst, a hall was booked in a northern town, and despite the greatest efforts of the company disaster loomed ahead when the week-end approached. It was obvious that receipts would nowhere near equal expenses ; after a frenzied whip-round it was found impossible even to collect enough to pay for the rent of the hall.

Mr. Morton, faced with a complete blank in bookings, and knowing that his company had not enough money in their pockets to keep them together any longer, went with a heavy heart to see the lessee of the hall.

It had been decided that, after their two years of agonizing effort, Maskelyne and Cooke would have to close down. The piano, the only bit of the properties worth anything in ready money, was to be left—if the lessee would generously accept it—in lieu of rent.

He proved to be a Quaker solicitor, of precise demeanour and businesslike speech. He greeted Mr. Morton civilly, and listened to his unhappy story. Then he sat silent for a few moments.

"Take thy piano with thee, friend," he said at last. "I do not attend theatres myself because of my beliefs. But we are told to be tolerant. I have heard excellent accounts of thee, William Morton, and of the young men Maskelyne and Cooke, whose work in exposing certain fraudulent persons seemeth to do much to protect the credulous and the afflicted. Take thy piano, and trouble no more about the moneys thou owest for the use of the hall. Go and prosper. Good-bye ; and God bless thee, one and all."

When Mr. Morton returned in jubilation to the saddened company, who were already saying their good-byes, he found a letter awaiting him from the manager of the Crystal Palace in London, offering him an engagement of several weeks there !

CHAPTER III

GOOD fortune never comes sparingly. While J. N., Cooke and Mr. Morton were still rejoicing in their reprieve from dissolution, the manager of a hall in a neighbouring town walked in and offered them an engagement for the next week. It was most useful to bridge the gap between then and the London engagement, but it nearly ended in tragedy.

I don't know whether the exhilaration of the future made the performances the following week a little *too* good. But by the Wednesday rumours were humming through the town that the conjurers were not illusionists merely, but magicians in league with the Evil One.

On that Wednesday evening a fiery old chapel preacher of the locality sat in the stalls. Grandfather took this as an enormous compliment, for chapels in the main did not then encourage the theatre in any of its branches. The best possible show was offered.

When the old man took his place in the stalls again the following night everyone was delighted. He set his stove-pipe hat fiercely beneath his seat, and seemed to settle down to enjoy the performance.

He came again on the Friday, accompanied by a couple of elders as cadaverous as himself. Grandfather hoped that some of the congregation might turn up on the Saturday— as a matter of fact, they had been playing to crowded houses since midweek.

33

Long before the Saturday evening show was due to begin it was obvious that the congregation *had* turned up. They were crowding and yelling and swaying outside the doors, hundreds strong ; and their tone left very little to be explained. They were out for blood.

In the forefront of the mob was the old preacher, waving a most unpleasant-looking stick and urging them on.

The manager of the place came in about a quarter of an hour before the performance was due to start. He was collarless, bloodstained and torn.

"Get out of here ! Get out of here !" he kept on repeating. "They'll pull you to bits, and my hall to bits on top of you. That old fool out there says you've been contracting with the devil. He's telling 'em now he's watched you these last three nights, and it isn't the magic of mortal man."

My grandfather was inclined to stay and let the matter settle itself, but in the company was his wife, and nothing on earth would have induced him to run a risk of her being harmed. They had married in Cheltenham when they were both very young—just before the first tour commenced, for she preferred to take her chance with him rather than wait for him to become rich and famous.

His first contract with Mr. Morton specified that he should receive £4 a week on behalf of himself and his wife and all his apparatus, while Mr. Cooke received £2 10s.

After some consultation, the manager went and rattled the bolts of the front doors of the hall, while the performers slipped away at the back.

Everyone, the manager included, retreated safely ; but there is no doubt that the mob, inflamed by the superstitions of the old preacher, were out for a lynching that night.

Fortunately, the receipts were such for the preceding days that not only was the rent of that hall paid, but the generous Quaker who had engaged them the previous week found his charges paid in full also.

1867! London! Or, at least, the Crystal Palace; for it was hardly accounted as London in those days. But still a wonderful step forward for the two lads who had started so boldly out of Cheltenham to give magic to the world.

Conjuring at this time was regarded rather in the light of a supplementary exhibition at a freak show! The Crystal Palace was famous for its freak shows, as was the Egyptian Hall, where Maskelynes later gained a real foothold in London.

And amazing exhibitions some of these freak shows were! They have gone out of fashion now, but I will quote you from a few of the old handbills of the time.

Valuable curiosities and living creatures collected by Mons. Boyle, late of Islington. They include a strange living Creature that bears a near resemblance to the Human shape in every part of his body but where decency forbids us to make mention of it; likewise an Oriental Oyster Shell of prodigious size; likewise the Philosopher's Stone, the size of a poulet's egg, which was clandestinely stolen from the Great Mogul's closet, this irreparable loss having so great an effect on him that he pined himself to death. . . .

To be seen at Mr. Boverick's, Watchmaker at the Dial, near the New Exchange in the Strand, at One Shilling each Person.

Or again :

A crane-necked carriage, the wheels turning on their axles, of ivory, together with six horses and their furniture, a coachman on the box, a dog between his feet, the reins in one hand, the whip in the other, two footmen behind, a postillion on the leading horse, all in proper liveries, and the whole so small as to be drawn along at a good pace by a flea. It has been shown to the Royal Family, and to several of the Nobility and Gentry.

Also a flea chained by a chain of 200 links, with a padlock and key, all wrought, the chain, flea, padlock, and key weighing together but one-third part of a grain.

Also a camel that passes through the eye of a needle; and a pair of steel scissors, able to cut a large horsehair, but six pairs can be wrapped in the wing of a fly. . . .

C

·It was among such curiosities as these, together with Siamese Twins, dwarfs, mechanical marvels, queerly shaped stones and automatic figures that the conjurer was thrown in as a make-weight to a sophisticated public.

My grandfather's show, therefore, unsupported by freaks of nature or art, depending for its effect on illusions and conjuring with nothing extraneous to divert bored attention, was very much in the nature of an experiment when a daring manager gave it a trial at the Crystal Palace.

The trial was an instant and unqualified success. J. N. produced his wonderful plate-spinning trick there for the first time. In it he spun about a couple of score of ordinary dinner-plates, one after the other, with inconceivable rapidity, and away they went, spinning down a four-inch-wide inclined gangway, and then round and round up a spiral, mounting the sides of a sort of miniature Eiffel Tower at the end, the total distance travelled being eight or ten feet, and the plates, one after another, climbing to a height two or three feet above that of the table-top from which they had set out.

A great sensation was caused by the first performance at this show of the now famous decapitation trick. Mr. Cooke sat in a chair facing the audience, well away from the backcloth, sides or any "properties".

J. N. then covered him with a shawl up to the neck, proceeded to cut his head off, removed the shawl—and there sat the headless trunk !

Subsequently, the "trunk" walked off the stage "with its head toocked oonderneath its arm" !

Last and most wonderful, J. N.'s wife, smiling demurely at the gaping spectators, stood free of scenery and curtains, and as the magician waved his wand she rose slowly into the air, with absolutely no visible means of support.

Since he was always willing to give thoroughly good

measure, J. N. then passed a metal hoop up and down round her body, to show that she was unsupported in any way whatsoever.

When the curtain rang down after that first Crystal Palace show it must have been a trying moment for the little band of performers. Their future would be decided by the response of that audience.

And then came the clapping ! It rose to shouting and stamping and cheering that would not be stilled. As J. N., with his arm round his wife's shoulders, pushed through the curtain to answer that urgent demand, he found himself, for the first time in his life, unable to say anything.

His fluency, his patter, his marvellous assurance so impervious to disappointment and failure—it had all gone. It was left to the little figure of his "assistant" to say, "Thank you, all ! Oh, thank you !" Then the cheering began anew.

The new fashion in conjuring had captivated London's fancy.

Night after night, before audiences that packed the Crystal Palace, the show gained fresh victories. The big newspapers began to send their representatives to report on what was fast becoming the talk of the town.

"They beat the spirits into fits !" acknowledged *The Times*, with unwonted levity.

The Davenports and their like faded into the background, making way for professional illusionists. But still there did not lack people who claimed that J. N. was a powerful medium, performing his wonders by means of spirit aid and then refusing to give credit to his ghostly helpers.

Others, more outspoken, said he was in league with the Devil ; and so the old legend reared its head again. But J. N. didn't mind ; he liked it ! It was wonderful publicity.

Before the end of that first Crystal Palace engagement he was putting back all the profits of the show into the construction of ever-improving apparatus for the production of magical tricks.

He made a walking-stick that lived up to its name, and walked about the stage unaccompanied. He performed variations of his decapitation trick that rendered onlookers breathless.

The ovation which London gave to the new show caused innumerable requests from the provinces for performances there. Mr. Morton found the big towns ready to welcome the magicians. Certain managers who had refused him with open contempt only a few weeks before when he *needed* bookings were now servilely anxious to engage the company.

To one, who had excelled his fellows in rudeness, the following answer was sent :

My dear Sir,.
We have received your offer to engage Messrs. Maskelyne
& Cooke's company for two weeks. Oh, my dear Sir !
Yours incredulously . . .

They played in that town, but at a rival establishment.

Considerable judgment was shown by Mr. Morton in keeping the show touring the provinces for several years now that steady bookings were available. He had seen many good performances put on in London before they were sufficiently experienced and mature, and after struggling on there for a year or two fade out again into provincial insignificance.

He and J. N. meant to go to London to stay when next they invaded the capital.

For no less than six years they increased their reputation in the big cities up and down England. New tricks were

steadily added to the repertoire, everything that the spiritualists did was faithfully reproduced without supernatural
assistance, and J. N. experimented more and more among
the wonders that could be presented by the aid of his
ingenious machines and devices, hundreds of which he
patented at this time.

In 1873 another appearance was made at the Crystal
Palace. Stimulated by the long absence of the show from
London, Society flocked to see the wonderful new magicians.

In addition to the tricks already famous, J. N. produced
some new ones for the occasion. His wife, radiant with the
memory of former successes there, acted again as his assistant. She rose into the air at his command, and floated there,
turning on her side and regaining an upright stance at will.

A bouquet was passed up to the stage in appreciation
of her turn. J. N. passed his wand over it, and it floated
across the stage by itself, and rose into her hand amid
thunderous applause.

Demure little Early Victorian as she was, the roses from
the audience almost hid her when the performance ended.

The time had come for the greatest venture of all. Early
in 1873 the company moved from the Crystal Palace into
London proper, appearing at the St. James's Great Hall in
Piccadilly for one month.

London took Maskelyne and Cooke to itself. Famous
people, gossips, Society ornaments and the *hoi polloi* came
in their thousands, and went away marvelling and anxious
to tell their neighbours about it.

A couple of engagements, booked some time previously,
were fulfilled at Croydon and Islington. Then, on May 26th,
1873, a three months' tenancy was commenced of the small
hall of the Egyptian Hall in Piccadilly.

The Maskelyne show was so different from anything
hitherto attempted in the conjuring line that rivals of

various sorts tried hard, during that initial three months, to drive the invaders back to the provinces.

A tremendous reception during the first week sharpened the jealousy that was already beginning to be openly shown. J. N. was branching out, engaging assistants outside the trio of himself, his wife and Mr. Cooke; and his rivals started their campaign by making friends with a minor magician who had obtained a job in the new company.

This man had to appear—or rather disappear—in the celebrated Box Trick. One night the opposition plied him well with liquor before he went on the stage.

He seemed sober enough, but trouble came later. In all disappearing tricks there is a cue to show that the vanishing has been successfully completed. Till this cue is heard the illusionist naturally dare not proceed with the trick.

No cue came. J. N. extemporized lines to fill the gap, but still there was no cue. Finally he had to open the box— and the man was lying inside in a drunken sleep.

J. N. told the audience that he would now vanish two men at once, since one alone seemed difficult. Mr. Cooke came on, got into the box, and was sealed and roped up. The drunken magician, whom J. N. pretended to have hypnotized to account for his stupor, was placed in a chair in the middle of the stage, and a sheet draped over him.

At a wave of the wand he vanished (with a bump, through a trap-door!) and Mr. Cooke disappeared from the box.

"Dr. Lynn", a famous magician then performing in another part of the Egyptian Hall, found the new show affecting his receipts. He brought an action saying that the new-comers were giving "dramatic performances".

The Hall was not licensed for such performances, and it was true that J. N. was already presenting magic playlets. But the attack failed; all it did was to bring valuable publicity.

The Egyptian Hall ceased, in public parlance, to be the

Egyptian Hall. It became "England's Home of Mystery"—
J. N.'s new name for his own section. Within the first three
months' tenancy Maskelyne's Magic had dwarfed all rivals
there into mere side-shows.

That three months' tenancy was extended. It lasted, in
the end, over thirty years, and was then only abandoned in
order that Maskelyne's might move to its own theatre,
St. George's Hall in Regent Street.

But J. N. would not rest on his laurels. He meant the
public to have ever-changing novelties, each more astounding than the last. And in the summer of 1873, when the
show had hardly been in London six weeks, there came to
see him one day a typical Lincolnshire farmer, slow in
speech and quiet in manner, who said he had something to
show that might interest a conjurer.

After an hour spent studying roughly drawn plans,
and listening to rather inconclusive explanations, J. N.
offered to go to Lincolnshire to see a mechanical man which
the farmer, a Mr. John Clarke, had invented.

On his return from the country J. N. went straight to
Cooke.

"I've discovered a bigger marvel than anything we've
made ourselves—so far," he said in great excitement. "It's
a mechanical man that can do arithmetic, spell and play
cards. I've guaranteed a very big price for it—more than
we can spend at present, but we must raise the money.
This thing is going to create a great sensation."

That was how the world-famous *Psycho* was born.

In order to perfect the farmer's invention, which was
nothing like the Psycho afterwards presented by my grandfather to an astounded London, J. N. opened a very large
workshop at the Egyptian Hall. This workshop was the
parent of the shops which have ever since provided about
sixty per cent of the vital essentials of all Maskelyne shows

right down to the present day. We have always been more mechanical illusionists than conjurers proper.

Psycho was a dwarf figure to which the face of a mild Hindu was later added. He had clockwork entrails, and was seated on a transparent glass cylinder.

J. N. worked steadily on that little figure for two years, and before that Mr. Clarke, the inventor, had put in years of spare time on its construction. When Psycho made his bow to the public on January 13th, 1875, he could nod, give the masonic grip, work extraordinarily intricate sums in addition, multiplication and division, perform minor conjuring tricks, spell, smoke cigarettes, and play whist.

He sat there, in the middle of the stage, without wires or tubes connecting him to anything extraneous, supported on his transparent pedestal, apparently perfectly detached from any connection whatsoever with human or outside mechanical assistance.

It was his whist that made him famous. He not merely played—he won ! In the course of many thousands—tens of thousands—of games, he lost less than a dozen times !

He played with most of the celebrated whist exponents of his time, including Mr. Cavendish, Dr. Pole, and "Trumps" of the *Field* newspaper.

Kings and Princes, as well as endless thousands of the general public, examined him and wondered at him. Other conjurers tried to duplicate him, and failed hopelessly. The nearest approach was *Cynthia,* exhibited at Sadler's Wells Theatre by Dr. Pepper, but it broke down, though it was infinitely less skilful than Psycho.

Psycho created a furore when he appeared in London. Racehorses, music-hall turns, overcoats and endless other things were named after him.

After innumerable performances in public, J. N. withdrew him, mainly because it was feared that his delicate mechanism might be affected by having worked for so long without a rest. He is in the London Museum now, and he could play a game of whist at any moment. Even to this day his construction remains a family secret.

Although J. N. paid a very good price for the original conception of Psycho, he was so delighted at its enormous success in public that he persuaded Mr. Clarke subsequently to accept a very fine present as some acknowledgment of the little whist-player's triumphs. The action was typical of the man.

But I have gone ahead of my story somewhat. Psycho, though J. N. began work on him in 1873, did not appear till two years later.

Meanwhile London flocked to the Egyptian Hall to see the box trick, the decapitation illusion, the mysteries of levitation, and all the other surprises that Maskelyne and Cooke could offer.

Mr. William Morton, who had "fathered" the show in its provincial days, and made possible its advent in London, was still manager, and remained so for many years. But Mr. Morton, who later became famous throughout England as a theatre manager, and who sponsored many of the most celebrated figures of our time, will forgive me, I know, if I say that already J. N. was emerging as the big figure of the company.

Mr. Morton, incidentally, is still alive, and is known, I think, to every man, woman and child in Hull, where he has now settled. He came to see a show of my own only the other day and sent me a letter of congratulation which I shall always treasure.

I will quote just one sentence from that letter. It reads: "I was glad to notice a carpenter's bench in your dressing-room."

The Maskelyne tradition, you see, still survives, and we are mechanics yet.

CHAPTER IV

Rival establishments—The spirits offer a partnership—A Royal Command Performance—Dr. Slade exposed—Zoe—Fanfair and Labial—A Royal birthday show—Mr. Cooke—J. N.'s commercial inventions.

WHEN Maskelyne and Cooke's show had been at the Egyptian Hall nearly a year, a spiritualist rival establishment set up business at the Hanover Square Rooms, in the person of a Miss Eva Fay. At first no supernatural aid was claimed by this lady, who was, incidentally, about the earliest real platinum blonde on record.

After a time, however, she advertised the fact that a familiar of the rather pleasant name of "Sweet William" produced the table-knocking and chair-movements on which her fame was based. She announced that William had been a carpenter by trade during his earthly life, and had him drive a nail into a piece of wood to convince any doubters, which, of course, was proof positive.

Surprisingly enough, J. N. still remained an agnostic. He and Cooke reproduced precisely on the stage at the Egyptian Hall every detail which William and his little blonde medium (assisted by her husband) could accomplish. But J. N. explained the workings of each trick as he did it. This gave the Hanover Square spooks a bit of a jolt. Miss Fay's business agent, who seems to have been almost human, wrote to my grandfather on May 12th, 1875, complaining that his principal was not properly supported by the Spiritualists, and offering, for a modest consideration, to expose the whole affair.   His letter read :

This will complicate (implicate?) at least six big guns. . . . Miss Fay is in the ring of all the best mediums in London, and gets letters every day that will be big to work upon.

J. N. apparently wrote in an interested strain, and in another letter, dated from Malvern on May 24th the same year, the business gentleman wrote what was obviously the spirit's last offer :

Some of the parteys that I named in my last to you are trying to persuade Miss Fay to go to America, and I am getin tired of messing about in this way. . . . I have another pretty young lady that I can bring out, and if I personely can will use all names and show the whole thing up as being the introducer of it to London.

The Old English form of spelling employed in these letters by the denizens of the other "spear" is quaint and interesting.

Miss Fay, finding the Egyptian Hall programmes affecting the cynical masses, was guided to go to America, while her business manager brought out the other pretty young lady as threatened, for a short and unsuccessful provincial season.

"England's Home of Mystery" at the Egyptian Hall flourished while its rivals withered.

A Japanese top-spinning trick, ventriloquism, reproduction of new spiritualistic phenomena, and similar novelties were added to the Davenport reproductions, levitation and decapitation. London flocked in endless crowds to see the new marvels.

On January 11th, 1875, J. N. received his first Royal Command for a performance of magic at Sandringham, before Prince Edward of Wales and Princess Alexandra, who were entertaining a distinguished party of guests there.

This was, I believe, the very first Command show of magic in a Royal presence since the days when jugglers were a recognized part of mediaeval Courts.

It was an enormous success! The Davenport Box Trick, with all its latest additions, was performed by my grandfather and Mr. Cooke. They wished a really elaborate and satisfactory performance to result, so they went to the trouble of taking movable scenery in considerable quantities with them, which was erected before the trick was given.

When it had ended the Royal party were so delighted with it that an encore was specially requested. But by this time, in readiness for the next illusion, scene-shifters had carefully backed from the Royal presence carrying the scenery and apparatus with them!

Of course everything had to come back and be set quickly into place. The Box Trick was then performed again, after which the scene-shifters once more picked up their unwieldy loads and backed, loyal but perspiring, out of the room.

Grandfather used often to tell us children this story, and to recount all the details of this first magic performance before the man who later became Edward VII. Of all the turns, the Prince and Princess applauded his plate-spinning trick most. And truly it looks big magic, for I have often watched Grandfather perform it for our amusement when I was a small boy.

The *Daily Telegraph* of the time commented on the extraordinary dexterity to which fingers can be educated, as demonstrated by this trick. When J. N. showed it to me, I remember, *he* presented the other side of the picture.

He told me he had smashed dozens and hundreds of plates in perfecting the turn, and created a heap of broken crockery that looked like a young mountain! He also said that it would be quite possible for a business man to educate *his* fingers and brains in his own affairs so that he could write two important letters simultaneously, one with each hand. American business hustlers, please copy—if they can!

At this time, and for the rest of his life up to within less than a month of his decease, J. N. worked twenty hours a day, and slept four hours.

This sounds impossible, but I know it to be true. He died "in harness" as a result, but I think he would rather have had it that way. I have never met such an indefatigable worker anywhere else.

He was in his workshops, experimenting with the apparatus for new illusions or whittling away at one of his innumerable non-theatrical inventions, at six o'clock in the morning, winter or summer. He worked all through the day, with brief stops for meals, either in the shops or on the stage rehearsing new illusions. He played in the theatre every afternoon and evening, and stayed up till two o'clock next morning dealing with business correspondence, arranging his affairs or puzzling out new turns.

But he was never too busy to accept a Spiritualist challenge. When Daniel Home practised a rather feeble sort of levitation at a séance, J. N. responded by floating a woman over the heads of the audience at the Egyptian Hall. When Charles Williams raised "the ghost of John King", J. N. exorcised a second and identical John King, who walked in spirit form the boards of the illusionist's stage.

Then, in July 1876, "Doctor" Slade set up in Upper Bedford Place, Bloomsbury, and began to raise the dead to some purpose. Dr. Slade introduced a new trick, that of persuading his ghostly friends to write on slates. J. N. sent to Dr. Slade a couple of slates so bound and sealed together that no human agency could unfasten them without leaving obvious marks—and asked the spirits to *write on the inner faces of the slates.*

This impious request was rightly refused. I have the slates to this day.

In due course Dr. Slade appeared at Bow Street police court, where he tried with notable unsuccess to convince Mr. Flowers, the magistrate, that there was nothing up his sleeve. J. N. was called as a witness, and demonstrated in court how it was possible to write on a slate, sponge out the words, and make them reappear there a short time later, as large as life and twice as natural.

There was a certain amount of laughter in the court when J. N. gravely explained that this trick was worked not by using a common slate pencil, but by employing a special stylo which he nominated a Slade pencil.

Dr. Slade was committed for three months' hard labour as a rogue and a vagabond, but his sentence was reduced on appeal. However, the spirits did not operate in London after that, apparently feeling disgusted at the vulgar reception of their marvels offered by learned exponents of the British law.

Since Psycho had been such an enormous success, J. N. had worked steadily on the production of other automata. In 1877 he proudly announced what he felt then was his masterpiece—*Zoe*, the charming little mechanical lady, who could sketch the profile of any celebrity chosen by the audience, and sketch it with the hand of a master of the pencil.

Zoe sat on a slender mahogany pedestal in the centre of the stage and held a pencil. A sheet of paper, on a drawing-board, was suspended in front of her. Before each performance, a committee of inspection from the audience was invited to come and examine the little lady, and discover, if possible, the secret of her powers. Needless to say, no one ever succeeded in doing that !

The *Morning Post*, welcoming the advent of Zoe, wrote :

Mr. Maskelyne, more complacent than Frankenstein, has created a Titania for his Oberon. Psycho is to be envied. A lovely companion, always smiling, never contradicting him, never troubling him about bills, or talking of the last sweet thing in bonnets ! As graceful as Angelica Kauffman, the mystery of her being is enhanced by the sheet of glass under the stand upon which she sits. A marvellous piece of mechanism, and does great honour to her maker, whose creative ingenuity is wholly without precedent, and seems to defy rivalry.

When Zoe was originally ready to "come out", J. N. suddenly hit upon a minor improvement for her, and her public appearance was delayed six months in order that, by infinite meticulous work, she could be made even more perfect than before.

Alas for human endeavour ! Zoe, rated by her creator as far superior to Psycho, was a comparative failure. Her sketches bore the impudent perfection of Whistler—but Psycho's whist held more elements of suspense. After a year or two of work, Zoe was ruthlessly withdrawn, because J. N.'s motto was always "The public knows what it wants !"

What a difference between this future holder of St. George's Hall and the B.B.C. who rule there at present !

The Maskelyne tradition of automaton wonders did not wane with Zoe. *Fanfair and Labial* made their bow in 1878. The former played the cornet, the latter the euphonium. They were scholarly little men, with the long locks and dreamy eyes of true musicians. One sat on a chair, the other on a music-stool. They were set in the middle of the stage, free from any connection with the sides, roof or—apparently—the floor, and they performed sweetly and accurately any popular piece of music asked for by the audience.

Highbrow or low, it was all the same to them. The audience could come up and examine them from every side. No works were apparent, no clockwork ticking or whirring was audible, there were no electric wires or air-pipe connections. There they sat, mysterious, complacent and earnest, and a good deal more human than some modern musicians I have met.

J. N. not only created all these various automata himself; he made their faces, their hair, their realistic hands and feet, inserted their teeth and eyelashes, superintended the very cut of their clothes. They were as much his children as were my father and uncle.

But why should I pay tribute to the musical twins and their mechanical confrères ? A. J. Phasey, solo-euphonium player to that exacting lady Queen Victoria, published in the *Musical World* of January 4th, 1879, a letter from which I might venture to quote :

> Labial's observance of light and shade filled me with wonder. . . . The lip-action is as perfect as with a human being; and, in his strict attention to the nuances, he was very far superior to many professional artists. . . . I sat close to the stage, to notice whether the fingering was correct or not. I found, to my astonishment, that the passages were not only correctly fingered, but that Labial introduced slurs and *appogiaturas* equally as well as any professor of the instrument.

The same year, 1879, J. N. received the signal honour of a Royal Command to appear at Sandringham as a special treat on the occasion of our late King's fourteenth birthday, on June 3rd.

By this time the Egyptian Hall show was one of the great attractions of London town. Country cousins were taken to see it ; a famous churchman of the time said publicly that he considered that no child's education was complete until he had been to England's Home of Mystery.

I wonder what the members of the original little Magic Circle at Cheltenham thought of it all ? They would have been family men by this time, some of them, and doubtless they took their children or their nephews and nieces to see Maskelyne and Cooke's when they were in London, and told them marvellous tales of the Davenport séance at

Cheltenham Town Hall, and how everything had really started from that.

In 1880, a new playlet was produced at the Egyptian Hall, under the appropriate name of *Cleopatra's Needle*. In this illusion, a small reproduction of the famous obelisk appeared on the stage, raised from the floor and free of all curtains and trappings. The temptations of St. Anthony were then represented in dramatic form, all sorts of figures emerging from the Needle, including the Devil himself; but the good Saint found that the last of them, none less than Royal Egypt herself, she who conquered that other and even more famous Antony from Rome, was the worst temptation of them all.

Mr. Cooke was in all these activities, of course, and was throughout his career in the firm an invaluable and loyal partner and a splendid magician. But he was by nature a shy and retiring little man, of small stature and apparently elastic bones, since his part was constantly to be fitted into incredibly small boxes, roped and sealed and nailed inside, and then spirited therefrom, answering from the gallery his colleague's call from the stage.

J. N.'s more powerful presence eclipsed him somewhat at times—indeed, there seems to have been a sort of general idea if Mr. Cooke was wanted that he had better be looked for in the nearest box ! But without his silent, unswerving encouragement and assistance, Maskelyne's could never have come into its own.

An illusion that caused a sensation at about this time was that of making a man out of his components. J. N. appeared on the stage carrying what looked like a bundle of arms, legs and general human assortments. These he dumped down on the floor, picking them up one by one and exhibiting them to show that each was genuinely separate from the rest.

D

Then he would take the trunk, clap a leg on to it—and, hey presto, the leg stuck! Then would come an arm, clad of course in the sleeve of a jacket, since each portion of anatomy was already dressed in the appropriate portion of garment. The arm was pushed against the trunk, and stayed in its place.

Another leg followed; then the second arm. The head, its eyes open and intelligent and its hair glossy and curling, was raised and stuck on to the neck of the trunk.

At this point J. N. waved his wand—and the figure began to speak in a human voice, to laugh, to slap its creator on the back; and finally, after adjusting its tie, it walked solemnly off the stage. It was obviously real.

One wonders what the body-snatchers of a rather earlier date would have said to this one!

During these years, theatrical success having been ensured in London, my grandfather began to turn his amazingly active brain to perfecting some of the innumerable inventions which, had he been lucky as well as ingenious, should have brought him a thousand times greater fame than even the best of his stage shows.

His first masterpiece was a typewriter, for which he devised, after much careful thought, the keyboard that has since been adopted as universal. It was then the only machine in existence with differential spacing of the letters from one another, so that a single line could hold, for instance, an average of twelve words, or of eighteen words, or of twenty-four words, the change being effected by a simple lever movement taking only a second to operate.

It had visible writing, could produce ninety-six characters, and was practically noiseless.

A public company was formed with a capital of £50,000 after this machine had finally been perfected. It was patented all over the world. It was, to my mind, as good as most of the modern typewriters of today. One of them, indeed, is still being used by a leading Streatham doctor. But the venture was a complete failure, and cost J. N. infinitely more than he ever got out of it.

In 1890, when typewriters were practically unheard of, he ran a typing office at the Egyptian Hall, where legal and scientific documents were typed for $1\frac{1}{2}d$. a folio, and authors' MSS. for 1s. per 1000 words.

. In writing of his inventions, I have to pick out for mention just a few of peculiar interest, since it is hopeless to enumerate them all.

He patented a means for operating gas-taps and electric switches, which was the forerunner of the present thermostatic control of which modern housewives are so proud when they have it fitted to gas or electric cookers.

In addition to having a value for such cookers, J. N.'s invention was devised so that electric and gas lights in streets and public buildings would turn themselves on or off at a set hour, as required. For houses, a further variation turned on the light in a room when a visitor opened the door and turned it out when the visitor left the room, unless the switch had been moved aside as when the light was needed throughout an evening.

Another patent concerned an improved method of joining railway metals, and would have greatly simplified points systems had it been brought into general use.

Yet another was a door-slot for the reception of pennies in public conveniences, and for chocolate machines, and similar automatic salesmen. This was almost unique among his inventions, in that it was successfully marketed, and it is to be seen to this day, still marked "Maskelyne Patent", on certain of our railways and river steamers.

Maskelyne's Checking Apparatus Company almost deserves a book to itself. When J. N. invented his automatic bus-ticket checker, there was nothing at all like it in existence, and it supplied a very real need.

The first checker consisted of an apparatus fitted over the entrance of buses, and it kept a complete and detailed record of all the business done by the vehicle in question. It showed how many passengers had been carried; how long the bus took over each stage of its journey; where passengers got on and alighted; how much each paid in fare; it protected the public from over-charge, and even registered if anyone got on the wrong bus and left without paying a fare.

To fit this device would have cost about £15 per bus; but the buses would have had to be changed slightly in build, and—there was nothing doing!

J. N. took the advice of the bus companies to try a cheaper device. He produced a wonderful little machine, and, over-persuaded by certain business men, sold the patent for £500 down and a royalty. The purchasers formed a public company with a capital of £50,000, and sold their shares like hot cakes on the strength of J. N.'s name.

He had refused to join the company himself. But on finding that the public had invested so heavily in it, and fearing that it would fail, he came in eventually, to try to make it pay by *giving* it the best work of his marvellous brain.

He invented another bus checker, took out all the patents at his own cost, and worked tirelessly to make it a commercial success. It was a device 2 in. by 6 in., was worn over the conductor's shoulder on a strap, and was worked by one hand.

The fare taken registered in a glazed aperture facing the passenger. Bells chimed the amount of each fare registered, striking once for each penny paid. A plain ticket was used for all values, the amount being perforated on it by the checker. The amount of the fare was registered on an index at the back of the checker, and the number of passengers carried and fares issued was registered on another index at the side.

All these operations were produced automatically by setting a pointer on the machine to the figure that represented the number of pence paid, just as is done now on the latest ticket-punch. The checker was simple, cheap to produce, and could be worked by a child. It was better than anything of the sort invented since.

Yet it failed to achieve public notice. No one would use it or purchase the patent. The company failed, despite my grandfather's efforts in its behalf—efforts that undermined his health very seriously, so fiercely did he pursue them.

All J. N.'s stage inventions were enormously successful. Every time he ventured out of the atmosphere of grease-paint and footlights he failed conspicuously, with the notable exception of certain work he did for the Government and War Office, which I shall detail later.

The same qualities that made him so supremely successful in his work as a public entertainer—sincerity, honesty and a burning desire to give the fullest value for the public's money—earmarked him as a lamb for the slaughter when he ventured into the more intricate realms of Big Business.

In the end, I think Big Business lost a lot more than it gained.

CHAPTER V

IT was about this time that J. N. first produced his famous playlet, *Will, the Witch and the Watchman*. This was intended chiefly as an amusing vehicle for the Box Trick that had so confounded the Davenports.

During his first years in London J. N. used to present the Box Trick following a short lecture on spiritualism and its conjuring supporters. But public opinion was already demanding something more dramatic and entertaining than a rather solemn lecture ; even in those days audiences went to the theatre rather to be entertained than to be educated, though the principle is not wholly accepted even yet.

But my grandfather, with his sensitive touch on the pulse of public desire, decided to scrap his lecture and build up round the Box Trick a little magic sketch with laughs and thrills all complete.

A cabinet built to represent an old-fashioned village lock-up was wheeled on to the stage. This lock-up was raised about a foot from the floor so that there was a clear space beneath it, excluding the possibility of a trap-door concealed in the stage below.

A big box with a canvas cover fitting over it, and a length of rope, were also brought on to the stage ; and a committee from the audience was invited on to the stage to examine both the lock-up and the box and accessories. Box and lock-up were clearly shown to be empty.

Some of the committees were so anxious to detect the working of the amazing tricks that followed that they deputed one of their members to lie full length on the stage with his head under the lock-up, staring upwards, while another would sit on top of the lock-up, and a third on a chair at the back. But none of them noticed any trickery, though they were often so eager to do so that they remained in their places quite oblivious to the play that was proceeding on the stage around them.

The rest of the committee took up positions on the stage wherever they wished—in front of the lock-up, behind it, at the sides or anywhere else selected.

Then Daddy Gnarl (my father) entered in the guise of an old squire, and a village Watchman accompanied him. There followed on to the stage a pair of young lovers, Will the Sailor and his sweetheart Dolly. Will was arrested for jollying the Watchman, and thrust into the lock-up, and his captor and Daddy Gnarl went off to celebrate the arrest in the usual fashion.

Meanwhile, the distracted Dolly sees an old woman (J. N. himself) creeping past, generously gives her a golden guinea, and is told that she is a Witch, who proposes in return to liberate Will.

The Witch causes a black monkey to materialize, and this animal goes off and annoys the Watchman, who returns to the stage in full chase, capturing both Witch and monkey, both of whom he places in the lock-up. But both the latter escape from and return to the lock-up as they wish, and the Watchman's shouts for assistance bring a butcher (also J. N.) on to the stage, who, in an effort to stab the monkey, slices off a bit of its tail.

This jumps about the stage on its own, much to the astonishment of the Watchman, who calls Daddy Gnarl back to help him. Meanwhile, the butcher shuts himself and the monkey into the lock-up. Opening the latter to see that the butcher is safe, Gnarl finds that Will, the butcher, and the monkey have all vanished, but the Witch is there.

The monkey is now seen hiding behind the lock-up, and is captured and forced into the big box. The committee from the audience then lock the box, keep the key, place the canvas cover over the box, lace it up, knot the lace and seal it, put a stout rope round the lot, and knot and seal that. The box is then placed inside the lock-up, and the latter closed and locked.

Gnarl, the butcher, and the Watchman are discussing their triumph when a hairy arm emerges and touches them from the lock-up. They fling open the door and lift out the box, still sealed, roped and laced, but so light that obviously the monkey is no longer within !

The Witch appears again with Dolly, and opens the door of the lock-up, which the audience had seen only a moment before quite empty. Will the Sailor is now standing inside it.

Under the influence of the Witch, whose powers none dare to cross further, the young couple are reunited and given the blessing of the entire party.

This sketch, which my grandfather performed over 11,000 times, was immensely successful, and was kept in the programme at intervals for over forty years ! I have often seen it performed. And though I know how it is done and have played in it myself, I am still stricken afresh with wonder each time I witness it.

The lock-up, raised from the floor, and with committee members sitting all round it intent on discovering "the works", produces figure after figure with bewildering ease and incredible speed, yet it can only just hold two persons at a time.

Once, in its early days, this trick caused a bit of a sensation. The action ran smoothly until the monkey was captured, and the committee were asked to imprison him. He was duly shut in the box, locked in, the canvas cover was laced up and roped, and the box was put in the lock-up.

The playlet ran on to the point where a cue should have shown the other actors that the monkey had left the box. But the cue was never delivered. With increasing anxiety and difficulty, the actors extemporized lines to cover the situation, waiting all the time for the missing cue.

As it did not come, they were forced eventually to open the lock-up and lift out the box. By its weight they instantly realized that the monkey was still within.

What had happened, in fact, was that *the monkey, before taking the stage, had found a whisky flask, emptied it, and then gone to sleep in the box.*

Without turning a hair, J. N. extemporized further lines to meet the situation ; the other actors followed his lead ; the playlet was lengthened a bit, to allow of the monkey being brought back on to the stage after a somewhat rude awakening—and then the rest of the act was played out perfectly according to programme !

The audience never realized that there had been a hitch.

Will, the Witch and the Watchman received a great welcome in England, where it was the first long magic playlet ever to be presented. But this was nothing to the furore it created in Australia, when a Maskelyne company was sent out to tour that country a few years later.

Such a sensation did it cause out there that the whole of the programmes for the tour had to be modified to include it at each performance. Its reputation went ahead of it, and at a mining camp in Western Australia, where by some accident the bills originally printed appeared with no reference to the new inclusion on the programme, a deputation of prospectors turned up and made a serious disturbance on the opening night.

A couple of dozen of them rose to their feet as soon as the curtain went up, and flourished revolvers. They were placed at strategic points all over the hall, and they shouted in unison : "Don't any of you move if you value your lives. We want *Will, the Witch and the Watchman*, or else we'll shoot up the stage."

There followed the crash of a revolver volley as they all fired together into the floor at their feet. Then, while the smoke still eddied about them, they all shouted in chorus : "Are you going to let us have it ?"

The brilliant young magician who was in charge of the illusionist side of the tour courageously stepped to the front of the stage, where he made a perfect target.

"You shall have it, boys !" he shouted ; and a tremendous cheer answered him.

The playlet was put on first in the programme, since the impatient miners were not in the mood to wait. A committee was invited from the audience as usual, and it tramped up on to the stage, revolvers, bowie-knives and all.

The lock-up was closed on this occasion by an old-fashioned padlock, the key of which was given to a burly prospector among the committee.

"We'll see there's no damned hanky-panky, fellars !" shouted this gentleman, waving the key at the audience ; and then he calmly put the key between his powerful yellow teeth and bit the end clean off; nipping through a quarter of an inch of cold iron to do so.

The act was greeted with a howl of delight ; but of course, when the door of the lock-up had later to be opened in accordance with the action of the play, a quandary arose. This did not deter the prospector, however. He simply went to the lock-up door, took the padlock in one enormous palm, thrust a stubby finger through the curved steel arc above the lock, and forced it free, using his finger as a lever.

After the playlet had finished, amid absolutely thunderous applause punctuated sharply by the constant crack of revolvers, Barclay Gammon, one of the finest entertainers who ever appeared under the Maskelyne or any other banner, gave a comedy interlude on the grand piano.

And there, as far as the official programme was concerned, the show ended.

The miners had never seen a grand piano before. Many had never seen a piano at all, except the cracked and broken-stringed ruin that decorated the local saloon ; and among these rough, often murderous, men there seems to have been an extraordinary sentimental love of music.

While *Will, the Witch and the Watchman* had been running the play had been almost submerged by a constant din of encouragement, laughter and comment. Now Gammon's first song was received in a startling silence.

With incomparable skill, the little entertainer assessed the spirit of his audience, and went straight into a second song, not a comic one this time, but a popular sentimental ditty of the era about home and love and beauty.

Having sung the first verse, he turned to the breathless audience.

"I want you all to join in the chorus, boys," he said.

They joined in, several hundred strong, blending their rough voices in a marvellous natural choir. When that song was done, first one and then a hundred voices demanded "Home, Sweet Home !"

For the rest of the evening, hours after the show was supposed to have finished, they were singing in chorus, one song after another. Towards midnight, the big miner who had bitten off the key-end yelled for silence.

"These boys want some sleep," he shouted. "We'll have one more song, and then pack up. What's it to be?"

All sorts of suggestions came crackling from various parts of the hall, but suddenly more and more voices blended demanding "Abide with me". The hymn was sung, reverently and splendidly, and then Gammon shut the piano.

He rose and stretched his cramped legs, meaning to leave the stage; but the next moment bags of gold-dust, coins, rings and money-notes were falling on the stage like a violent hailstorm.

After that, the arrangements for the tour had to be changed again. At camp after camp in Western Australia the magic show was turned into a sing-song that sometimes lasted for five or six hours at a stretch. The grand piano became the star of the tour, and *Will, the Witch and the Watchman* took a close second place. Other illusions were crowded out, though they had been carefully rehearsed for months beforehand.

Slowly passing on its way through the southern continent, Maskelyne's show travelled by ox waggon and on horseback over thousands and thousands of miles. Performances were given in gambling saloons and in tents; the only available lighting was usually by means of candles. Contractors with dozens and hundreds of empty boxes, formerly containing bully-beef or explosives, used to hire out their primitive seating at prices sometimes rising to £3 and £4 a box.

Often enough, a good part of the audience was coloured; not only Australian Blackfellows but Chinese, negroes and half-breeds of every shade and description.

Applause was generally marked by revolver salvos; and had the entertainers displeased their audiences the probability is that the revolvers would have been turned on them. However, amazing offerings of gold-dust and other such tokens of appreciation followed nearly every performance in the back-blocks.

The piano and *Will, the Witch and the Watchman* remained firm favourites ; and nearly all the shows were ended with sing-songs in which everyone joined. It was an astonishing and tremendously successful tour.

It was shortly after the conclusion of this tour that my grandfather conducted his short and startling campaign against card-sharpers and gambling swindlers in Great Britain.

At that time the country was overrun with these gentry to a degree that has never been even remotely approached since. The general public was not then aware—indeed, I doubt whether it is so to this day—how ridiculously easy it is for a skilled operator to change most card games from chance to certainty ; and J. N., with the same inherent hatred of swindling that inspired him against the Davenports, Miss Fay and others, rushed into a single-handed campaign against the "sharps" of his day.

At the same time he inaugurated a rule which holds good among all Maskelynes to this day—that none of us shall ever play cards for money. The reason is that our magic knowledge would automatically engender suspicion against us.

If you gave me, for instance, any selected card from a pack whose seals you had just broken, and let me examine the back of the card for only a couple of minutes, and then examine the backs of the rest of the pack, I would defy you to shuffle that pack as you liked, and I would then draw out your selected card, wherever it might be among the rest, within ten seconds or so, only examining the backs of the cards the while.

It is not even now generally known that very many packs of cards used in England are so printed that some almost

imperceptible variation on the back marks the face-value
of each card to a trained eye. It may be that a minute portion
of scroll-work turns right to indicate a King, left for a
Queen, upright for an Ace, and so on. Perhaps it is a variation in the glaze of the back; or perhaps a hairbreadth
difference in the squareness with which the corners
are cut.

Almost always, the difference is there, and can be
detected. After that, the well-informed player knows just
what cards are held by his opponents, since suits are often
indicated also. And then, of course, the money staked on
the game is his for the taking.

Many years ago, one of the most colossal frauds the
world has ever known was undertaken by a brilliant card-
sharper of the name of Bianco.

At the time, Havana was the gambling-ground of the
world, and it was to Havana that Bianco went. Having
purchased in Spain about thirty thousand packs of unused
playing-cards, he opened every pack, marked every single
card in a manner only detectable to himself, and resealed
the packs in such a way that they seemed perfectly intact.

He had marked the cards not only in values, but in
suits. Then he set himself to learn the complicated system
of markings he had employed so that he could use it fast
enough to control by its means the quickest of card-games,
and so that he could detect by casual glances exactly what
cards others were holding without arousing suspicion.

This training took him over a year of intensive study
and practice; and he admitted no associate to his plans.
During this period, too, he "cornered" the entire playing-
card trade of Havana by offering his marked packs—which
were good and expensive cards—at less than half the price
usually charged.

So successful was he that Havana dealers bought from

him exclusively, since no one else could offer them good cards at anything approaching Bianco's price.

The sharp himself followed his cards to the island, and settled down to make a fortune. His amazing memory enabled him to carry out his scheme to perfection. Wherever he played, the cards were ones he had marked; he allowed himself to lose occasionally, but vast sums of money went his way between these spells of chosen ill-fortune.

Alas for Bianco ! The best-laid plans are not always fool-proof, and it was a man with the reputation of a fool who found him out. Alys de Laforcade, ci-devant Count of the old French regime, was considered in Havana a charming man but lacking in shrewd common-sense.

This young man, however, became so friendly with Bianco that he accompanied him to and fro about the island ; and presently, having studied his methods, gently broke the news to his Spanish friend that the secret by which Dame Fortune was so successfully propitiated had become his property also.

Bianco asked him what he proposed to do about it. The ci-devant Count could hardly have been such a fool as he looked, for he suggested introducing Bianco to the most exclusive clubs and households of the island—places to which the Spaniard's eyes had eagerly turned ever since the opening of his golden campaign.

De Laforcade professed himself delighted to aid his charming acquaintance—for a price. Such a simple little price. Merely fifty per cent of the proceeds, with none of the work and none of the risks.

It says something for Bianco's takings that he accepted the terms without much demur.

And so the adventurer began a new phase of his meteoric career. The oldest and most exclusive society of Havana greeted him, and played for high stakes with him.

The French nobleman, hitherto genteelly impoverished, explained with his delightful simper, to all who would listen, that his dear maternal grandfather, a Spanish nobleman, had just regrettably passed away, yet had had the forethought to leave his worthless scion his entire fortune.

De Laforcade took a splendid house, entertained royally (and played cards occasionally), got together a stables that was the envy of the island, and established an almost world-wide reputation as a dilettante in wine, women and pleasure.

At the height of his fame, Bianco vanished (having for over a year "cooked the books" of the infamous partnership to an amazing degree, since naturally de Laforcade could not check the takings), and the Frenchman was left enormously in debt.

This his sensitive soul might have borne, but in addition irrefutable evidence reached the society of Havana that he was a card-sharper, and that his fortune had been amassed by his play rather than from his Spanish relative. He was brought before the Tribunal, the whole story of the marked cards came to light (but with de Laforcade playing the principal role and Bianco not even mentioned), and after a long case the Frenchman was acquitted, because it could not be proved that he had imported the cards himself. He dared not mention Bianco for fear of thus admitting his own guilt.

However, his name, fame and fortune were broken, and he died miserably not long afterwards, while Bianco was last heard of as a great and pious patron of the Church in his own beloved Spain.

I do not think that anyone of the skill and energy of the late-lamented Mr. Bianco has ever operated in England, though there have been queer dealings here at times, as is testified by the fact that King Edward VII, when Prince of Wales, went into the witness-box to defend the reputation of a friend of his who had been accused of cheating at cards.

But certainly, in my grandfather's time, the country was riddled with clever sharps, and his brief but decisive campaign to expose them must have done them enormous harm, and crippled their activities for many years.

He explained in newspapers, at lectures and in a fascinating book entitled *Sharps and Flats*, all the principal methods of swindling, and dealt in full with the mysteries of marked cards, hold-outs, reflectors, dice, collusion, race-gangs and several other kinds of swindle.

He made it abundantly clear—though the fact has since been forgotten by the public—that several big firms, both in England and America, exist largely by reason of their sales of the complicated apparatus used by card-sharpers.

This includes clips and wrist-bands for holding high cards secretly removed from the pack ; machines for marking, squeezing, clipping and roughening valuable cards ; ready-marked packs, weighted dice, clipped coins guaranteed to fall always the same way up on being spun, faked roulette outfits ; secret mirrors for use at cards ; acid for shading the backs ; coat machines for card manipulation, and a hundred other devices for the undoing of the unwary.

J. N. also exposed the innermost secrets of the way in which sharping gangs work, playing in combination to rob innocents and sharing out proceeds afterwards, spending years studying legerdemain and manipulation, having their agents at the Universities, in the City, on the Riviera, on all long-distance liners and trains, and often going through a course of training which makes them as skilful in conjuring and illusion as most of the professional magicians who appear on the stage.

Even today card-sharping and similar methods of plucking the down from the unfledged are highly organized

E

professions with world-wide ramifications. Any retired liner skipper can tell you that the gangs that work the Atlantic, for instance, make fabulous fortunes, and are well-known to one another, and to stewards and detectives on both sides, though they are mostly too sharp to be caught doing anything illegitimate.

I have not space in this book to go at all fully into the subject of what one might call card-magic, but at least I can warn readers against that elementary and yet immensely lucrative hoax, the three-card trick, commonly known as "Find the Lady".

A stranger comes into a railway carriage, and other members of his gang drift in later, none apparently being known to any other. The sharper gets out a pack of cards "to while away the journey", selects three, one of which is a Queen, shuffles them face-down, and invites anyone present to pick out the Queen.

First one confederate and then another selects the Queen quite successfully, after repeated shufflings ; and finally one of them puts a shilling on his choice, and wins. The dealer loses about nine times out of ten until some greenhorns are drawn into the game by the apparent ease with which money can be made at it.

Now, by a simple bit of legerdemain, the dealer varies his handling of the cards, and the Queen is never the card selected by the greenhorns. Stakes are raised as high as possible before the innocents enter the game ; after that money changes hands with tremendous celerity.

The great attraction of the trick is that no one not in the secret can believe that his eye has deceived him until the selected card is turned face-up ; it seems as if the eye has never left it since it was turned up previously, and that it *must* be the Queen.

That it is not, in the event, thousands of astonished

travellers who have been swindled in this way can testify, up and down the length of Britain.

A variation of this trick, painfully well known to almost all Americans, which has recently become somewhat of a feature on our own fair-grounds, is that in which a pea is hidden under one of three walnut shells, and the gambler is invited to put his money on the shell which he thinks hides the pea.

This trick was first presented on the stage by Harry Kellar, one of the cleverest magicians of all time.

Kellar became famous while touring with an illusionist company near his home in Pennsylvania. In 1868 he joined the Davenport Brothers, but as a magician, not a spiritualist. Later on he came to London, where he threw himself with extraordinary vigour into the production and staging of some clever automata.

He started with an imitation of my grandfather's "Psycho", but it broke down frequently, and could only perform elementary tricks. Nothing daunted, Kellar introduced "Echo" and "Phono", two mechanical musician figures that directly copied J. N.'s "Fanfair" and "Labial", but could not play a tithe of their repertoire, and were also subject to frequent irritating periods when they went on strike altogether.

"Clio" was his next attempt ; an automaton that was produced in rivalry to my grandfather's "Zoe", the drawing figure. But "Clio" was not much of an artist, and had a very short life in London.

Despite his ill-success with automata, Kellar was a most accomplished illusionist and conjurer, and held for many years in America the position that J. N. did in England.

His natural successor in the art of card-manipulation on the stage was Howard Thurston, another American magician. He joined forces with Kellar, and built up a great reputation with an infinite variety of brilliant card tricks, and later with some very fine and startling illusions. In a recent American book on magic I saw myself referred to as "The Thurston of England". I can hardly do less than pay this accomplished magician the return compliment, and call him the Maskelyne of America.

CHAPTER VI

MASKELYNE AND COOKE's, with only a few years between them and their struggling provincial days, took the bold step at about this time of sending touring companies of magicians round the big towns of Great Britain. One of the first places visited was Cheltenham, where doubtless the show created a good deal of sentimental interest.

J. N. went in person with his first touring company to visit Ireland. He always preferred to break new ground himself; and on this occasion his fancy nearly involved him in serious trouble.

On the opening night in Dublin, where the company was engaged for a five weeks' season by Messrs. Guinness, the brewers, who were then running a big exhibition in the Irish capital, a member of the audience objected pointedly to J. N.'s opening speech.

"Shut up your bloody preaching and get on with the magic!" came a yell from the gallery.

Instantly came back the answer: "I'm getting on with it! I'm trying to make you disappear—for the benefit of your immediate neighbours!"

During this Irish visit, feeling ran very high against England and all things English. On the evening of May 6th, 1882, as J. N. was strolling through Dominion Street on his way to the theatre he saw a couple of young roughs race past him and disappear down a side-turning ahead. They carried revolvers, and glanced fearfully back as they ran. My grandfather always believed that these two men were the murderers of Lord Frederick Cavendish, who was shot that evening while walking in the adjacent Phœnix Park, and that they were then running from the scene of their crime.

Later in the same visit, J. N. was in a street somewhere near the Four Courts when some prison vans passed him guarded by mounted police. A great mob followed, jeering and yelling and throwing bottles and stones at the police, who turned and charged them two or three times.

The magic show, however, did not suffer at all from the anti-English demonstrations. Every night the seats were packed, and despite some crude chaff and shouting the audience seemed thoroughly satisfied with the performances.

By this time Maskelyne had become a great name in the world of magic. Illusionists famous not only in England, but abroad, commenced to approach J. N., seeking the honour of appearing under his management.

One of the first whom he accepted as an assistant was Charles Bertram, one of the most handsome men ever to appear on the stage. Bertram was popular wherever he went. He appeared no less than twenty-two times before King Edward VII, and also gave innumerable performances of magic at the houses of celebrities and nobilities.

He may be said to have initiated the practice of giving illusionist shows at private parties at Christmas and other times—a form of magic demonstration which keeps me very busy nowadays, and which sometimes causes me to give three or four shows a day in addition to my stage performances.

Bautier de Kolta was one of the cleverest magicians who ever joined Maskelynes. He was very famous when

he came to the Egyptian Hall in 1875, in direct competition
to Grandfather and Mr. Cooke. Eleven years later he joined
J. N.'s company, bringing with him a very pretty illusion
which he entitled "The Vanishing Lady".

In this trick a small mat was placed on the stage and on
it a lady sat in an ordinary small chair. The mat precluded
any possibility of a trap-door beneath her being used for
her subsequent disappearance, yet disappear she did the
moment a cloth was draped over her. De Kolta whipped
away the cloth almost as soon as he had arranged it ; but
the lady was gone.

J. N. bought this illusion from de Kolta, and also
purchased the chair in which it was first performed. That
same original chair was used recently by Miss Gracie Fields
in making her charming talkie, "Sing As We Go", and
Gracie vanished as suddenly and surprisingly in that film
as did the original disappearing lady fifty years ago.

For some years de Kolta and Bertram were very popular
figures at the Egyptian Hall. Not all their tricks, however,
went off without a hitch.

On one occasion Bertram was performing a clever bit
of conjuring when "something went wrong with the
works", and the result cost my grandfather nearly £1000.

A big diamond ring had been borrowed by the magician
from a lady in the audience. Bertram put the ring in an
ordinary envelope, sealed it, set fire to a corner of the
paper, allowed the envelope to burn away to ashes—and
the ring had disappeared.

He then made a big paper cone, showed it empty to
the audience, doubled over the end, and lo ! the paper cone
began to move convulsively. Bertram opened it up, and
there inside was a live dove, with the ring fastened about
its neck by means of a piece of blue ribbon.

According to theory, the dove should have circled

round above the heads of the audience, returned to Bertram's hand, and allowed the ring to be detached from the ribbon and returned to the owner. On this occasion, however, someone had foolishly left open one of the theatre ventilators.

The dove flew straight to this ventilator, slipped through it, and flew out into the world, with the £1000-ring still round its neck!

Of course there was a hue and cry, particularly from the lady when she found that her wonderful ring had vanished so realistically. Stage hands were sent rushing out into the streets to try to locate the dove. Inside the theatre mild pandemonium reigned. But the dove was never seen again —at least, not by its rightful owners. J. N. had to recompense the loser of the ring, and get as much advertisement as he could out of the affair as it stood.

Charles Morritt, Edward Longstaffe, James Stuart, Sidney Oldridge and many other clever magicians became famous at about this time, and most of them appeared at one period or another under J. N.'s triumphant banner.

A most interesting member of the conjuring fraternity who joined Maskelynes in the last decade of last century was Douglas Beaufort. In addition to being one of the finest illusionists of his age, Beaufort was a man of remarkable personality and great gifts.

During his career he was selected by the British Foreign Office to accompany Sir Charles Ewan Smith and the British Mission to Fez, there to give a series of performances before Mulai el Hassan, the Sultan of Morocco. Already there were murmurs of coming trouble in North Africa, which later came to a head in Egypt, the Soudan and elsewhere. It was vital to us at the time to secure the friendship of Morocco.

France, which had rival interests in Africa, had, so it was said at the time, added beauties to the Sultan of

Morocco's harem, and had given him a little hand-movie apparatus that showed Paris night-life at its gayest. So England replied by sending out Mr. Beaufort and his magic to charm the royal heart into an even greater sympathy towards Great Britain.

In travelling from the coast to Fez, the Sultan's capital, the illusionist gave some impromptu performances. The Arabs had never seen magic of this sort before, and so greatly did it outshine the efforts of their own snake-charmers, jugglers and marabouts that an enormous reputation preceded Mr. Beaufort to the Royal Court.

Indeed, too much success almost defeated its own ends ! For sick and maimed people *en route* were carried to see the new "Devil Man", as he was respectfully called, and, some of these growing better because Nature and their faith willed it so, the illusionist suddenly developed the proportions of an almost national figure.

As a result, when he reached Fez the Sultan was altogether too frightened to see him at all !

For eight weeks the dusky royalty lurked furtively within the Palace confines lest the visiting magician should cast a spell over him. Finally, however, curiosity got the better of his fear.

A great gala performance was arranged to take place before the Sultan and his whole Court within the precincts of the Palace. The place chosen adjoined the royal harem, and was patrolled at night by three powerful lions, which had never been tamed, and would have attacked an intruder on sight.

While Mr. Beaufort was preparing for his performance, three or four of the royal ladies slipped swiftly round a portico into a hidden corner, to try to watch the proceedings. But a black eunuch saw them and advanced on them, beating them savagely about the shoulders with a heavy stick, and driving them back to the seclusion of their own quarters.

The Sultan, surrounded by over a score of his sons and all his chief Ministers, finally took his place on the throne and nervously indicated that Mr. Beaufort should begin.

At first, the dark-skinned ruler was so nervous that he showed signs of fright as each trick approached its climax. But soon he was absolutely fascinated by the performance, and watched with his mouth half-open in sheer astonishment.

Once the illusionist advanced towards the Sultan so that he could watch closely the performance of a rather intricate trick. His Majesty shuffled to his feet, looked round for an avenue of escape, and held out his hands as if to ward off the conjurer's approach.

Later, however, gaining courage, he suddenly swept down from his place, advanced to Mr. Beaufort, and hoarsely commanded him to produce a handful of living snakes from his mouth.

For a moment the reputation not only of the visitor, but of England, was at stake.

"Englishmen despise snakes, Your Majesty," was the quick-witted reply. "We have no dealings with them, and consider them unclean. But I will do something even more wonderful—I will produce a great number of eggs from the mouth of your own interpreter!"

The Sultan was more than satisfied. As egg after egg came neatly from the mouth of the official named His Majesty stepped nearer and nearer and repeated in a hypnotized voice: "More! More! More!"

The climax of the performance was reached when the illusionist gave an exhibition of ventriloquism, of which he was a master. So certain was the Sultan that this was the work of confederates that he had the Palace precincts searched ; and each time a voice sounded from behind a hanging or beside a pillar, a huge negro soldier armed with a drawn scimitar ran to the spot ; and it would have gone hard, probably, both with the assistants and himself had Mr. Beaufort's trick not been genuine ventriloquism of the highest order.

At the end of the show, the Sultan, who was in tremendous glee, ordered that the magician should sing to him !

A difficulty arose. No European singer could give a satisfactory performance accompanied by the zithers and tambourines of Morocco, yet the one and only piano in Fez was in the Palace of Kaid Harry Maclean, the Scottish Commander-in-Chief of the Moorish Army, who was present at the time, and his home was over a mile away.

However, Mr. Beaufort decided to sing unaccompanied, and rendered a laughing-song so satisfactorily that the Sultan—who did not understand a word of it—joined in so heartily that he laughed himself into tears !

At the end of the performance he presented his entertainer with a marvellous Arab horse of incredibly ancient pedigree from his own stables, a silver dagger and a bag containing five hundred dollars.

Mr. Beaufort, who is still an active figure in London, gave no fewer than ten performances before the late King Edward VII, and has at one time or another appeared before nearly every member of the Royal Family, besides touring in Australia, South America and South Africa. Yet he still declares that the hardest audience to satisfy is one composed of British schoolboys. He says they have eyes like gimlets ; and what they fail to see, they explain away with perfect *sang-froid*, though usually their explanations are miles from the truth. This, however, does not disturb them !

After his return from Morocco, Mr. Beaufort and my grandfather got together and devised a magic playlet, incorporating some of the events of the African visit, which was staged at the Egyptian Hall, where it was an enormous success, and ran for over two hundred performances.

To my mind, the most amazing thing about this journey to Morocco—which, by the way, had most satisfactory political repercussions later, and made the Sultan the friend of Britain for the rest of his life—was the nerve that must have been required to produce illusions under such conditions. In those days, it was a very wild country where the Sultan's whims were law and his word carried the power of life and death.

It is not at all unlikely that the slightest hitch or hesitation in any of the tricks performed in the Sultan's presence might have resulted in frightening the dusky ruler, and causing the magician to be imprisonerd, or even perhaps put to death in an access of royal terror.

A comparatively unknown magician who started his astounding career at the Egyptian Hall under J. N.'s banner was an Irishman who worked at the time under the name of John Malone.

This man conceived the enterprising idea of abandoning the English stage, where he might well have made a great name, and touring as a free-lance performer through the East, the legitimate home of magic.

He travelled through India with amazing success, and there took the name of Prester John, because of its associations with the famous legendary Eastern King, who was also supposed to have been a white man. Malone said he was a reincarnation of this ruler; and that claim, together with his genius for magic, gained him a colossal reputation.

Later he toured through Arabia, Asia Minor and Turkey.

In the latter country he came by a strange adventure that came near to ending his life, but concluded by redoubling his fame.

He incurred the enmity of a holy Marabout, who was himself a famous magician, and this man caused "Prester John" to be haled before the Sultan of Turkey, where that august potentate ordered a "trial by miracles" between the two.

The Marabout's first trick was to hypnotize a snake (as Moses did before Pharaoh) till it grew straight and rigid, and cast it on the ground, when the shock "brought it to life" and it wriggled away. The Irishman, being no hypnotist, could not equal his rival's magic in that particular. Nor could he compete with him in the next illusion he presented before the Sultan and a superstitiously muttering Court—that of growing a dwarf date-palm from a date stone in a matter of minutes, and plucking fruit from the palm which had grown there before the beholders' very eyes.

"And now we will see *your* magic, white man!" said the Sultan in a menacing tone.

"Prester John" craved permission to have brought to him one of his trunks, which he said contained a potent preparation that would prevent him from being harmed in the great feat that was to follow. He also asked that a Turkish youth, whom he had cured from fever long before and who had since served him as a valet, should be brought before the Sultan.

The box was set down some yards from the throne, and the courtiers drew back, fearing too close an experience of the coming magic. The Turkish boy then lay down on his face on the box, and "Prester John" solemnly covered his assistant's head with a cloth. He felt under the cloth for a minute or two, muttering incantations, and then withdrew the cloth.

The boy's headless body lay on the box, with a blood-stained knife beside it; in the Irishman's hand, held by the long hair, its eyes staring horribly and its neck still dripping blood, was the young Turk's head!

An exclamation of horror ran round the place, and the Marabout began a wild accusation that his rival had committed murder in the Sultan's sacred presence. But the Irishman fiercely commanded him to be silent lest he be blasted into dust.

Then, after walking to and fro holding up the dripping head, "Prester John" strode back to the corpse, covered the neck and shoulders with a cloth, thrust the decapitated head beneath it, worked for a minute or two—and withdrew the cloth, whereupon the lad, his head now in its rightful place, stood up, spoke, walked about, and showed that he was whole and undamaged.

The priest who had dared to accuse such a dread magician was cast by the Sultan into a dungeon beneath the Bosphorus, there to await his ruler's pleasure. "Prester John", however, was offered an important position near to the Sultan's person, and a great gift of gold, jewels and women, all of which he is said to have accepted without demur.

After that, this amazing Irish magician vanished in a whirling mist of legend.

His illusion of the decapitated youth was performed by the aid of an invisible trap-door in the box on which the lad lay.

He thrust his head down through this trap-door after "Prester John" had withdrawn from inside the box a dummy duplicate head previously prepared against just such an emergency. On the back of the boy's neck, the magician applied a little wet dough paste, and a smear of red ink, to give the impression of a severed neck. The dummy head was similarly ornamented. Finally, the dummy was returned to its place in the box, the boy withdrew his head, "Prester John" cleaned the paste and ink from his neck, and withdrew the cloth after closing the trap-door.

The superstitious dread of the Sultan's Court kept them from coming near the great white magician; and, except at very close quarters, the trick is undetectable.

In 1893, that distinguished magician Mr. David Devant joined Maskelyne's company, and inaugurated a new phase in the history of the family. Starting with a three months' contract at a small salary, he subsequently became so much a part of the firm that he was given a partnership, and Maskelyne and Cooke's became Maskelyne and Devant's, under which latter title it flourished for many years and owed to the new-comer much of the fame it achieved in subsequent times.

Towards the end of last century, the workshops where my grandfather and his associates prepared the apparatus for their ever-increasing list of illusions became so extensive as almost to dwarf that part of the Egyptian Hall devoted to public performances of magic. Some amazing and intricate apparatus was produced and patented. Nor was this solely devoted to the art of conjuring.

J. N. became interested in a device which held promise of being able to fill balloons with gas much more quickly than had been done up to that date. Together with Professor Bacon, he worked for over two years perfecting this apparatus, and obtained such recognition for his work that the War Office approached him to undertake some experiments in connection with the filling of military observation balloons.

These experiments were successful, and much useful work was done, the results being utilized by the British Army during the South African War. J. N. also experimented with apparatus for ascertaining the speed of sound in connection with the firing of big guns, but was not so successful in these researches as he was with his balloons.

By this time, his son Nevil was helping him, both in the workshops and on the stage. My grandfather had two sons, Nevil (my father) and Archie. Nevil took to the illusion business as if born to it, and even followed tradition by marrying a lady connected with the profession. Mr. Devant did likewise, marrying a lady who worked with him in some of the prettiest illusions ever invented ; and in due course I myself followed the same road by marrying my "vanishing lady", as I shall recount later. Surely there must be strong magic somewhere to account for such a succession of coincidences.

It was Mr. Devant who was responsible for obtaining for the Egyptian Hall some of the first movie-picture shows ever seen in England. Little did anyone guess then that the novelty to which a few minutes of the Maskelyne pro-gramme was devoted each evening was subsequently to oust conjuring to a very great degree from public interest, and to contribute largely towards the condition of things which eventually caused Maskelynes' Theatre to be taken by the B.B.C.

In 1896, Lumière brought an "animated picture" show to the Polytechnic Theatre, and after some negotiation with my grandfather offered him a machine to show these pictures at the Egyptian Hall at a hire price of £100 a week —a very large sum in those days. The demand was, in fact, too high.

But an English inventor of the name of Paul had simul-taneously produced a similar machine, and Mr. Devant, finding Mr. Paul eventually in the midst of negotiations with a rival manager, bought the invention for £100, which he paid out of his own pocket, in order to secure the marvel for Maskelynes' show. Two days after Lumière started showing his "movies" at the Empire Theatre, where the general public saw them for the first time (the previous show having been for theatrical managers only), Maskelynes were filling the Egyptian Hall for shows with Mr. Paul's invention.

Meanwhile, the workshops behind the stage were busier than ever, for J. N. and his son Nevil were now taken up with the problem of devising an apparatus that would run movie films continuously and smoothly. The two of them spent months trying to overcome the difficulties that faced them in this task, but never succeeded to their own satisfaction.

Films were taken of public events, such as Queen Victoria's Jubilee, and so I think Maskelynes can claim the credit of producing the first news-reels on record. They also filmed the first pictures ever made of theatrical performances, though, they did not unfortunately hit on the golden idea of filming complete plays and offering them to the public as movies or talkies.

Still, several films were made of J. N., Nevil Maskelyne and Mr. Devant, together with my aunt Cassie Maskelyne, and others, performing little magic playlets or producing illusions. These pictures were "shot" on the roof of the Egyptian Hall in the closing years of last century, and were extensively sold all over England and America, where perhaps they stirred a germinating ambition in the mind of some Laemmle or Korda whose fame was yet unborn. Queen Alexandra sent a special request for some of the pictures taken of herself and other members of the Royal Family at a Chelsea Hospital fête, and many other distinguished people in England began to take an interest in the new art.

At this time, J. N. issued a challenge throughout England that created a great sensation. Briefly, he offered £1000 to

the first person who could do the two following things :
(1) prove that he had discovered the secret of the famous
Maskelyne Box Trick, and (2) produce a box and duplicate
with it the tricks J. N. himself would do with *his* box at a
public performance.

In 1898 this challenge was accepted. No agreement was
reached as to whether the challenger correctly imitated my
grandfather's trick, and eventually the case came into Court.
The jury disagreed, after examining J. N.'s original mystery
box and its rival in the presence of the Judge, and the case
came before a fresh jury. There seems no doubt that the
claimant never explained the secrets of the original box,
whatever he may have done in the way of reproducing the
trick himself, and so failed to comply with the first condition
of the challenge ; but the case, after dragging right up to
the House of Lords, was finally awarded against my grandfather, who had to pay the £1000 he had offered.

With a pugnacity typical of him, he immediately revived
the Davenport box trick on the stage at the Egyptian Hall,
and engaged some topical *notabilia* to perform in it. In this
way he made far more money than he lost over the case.

It was one of J. N.'s gifts that he always knew when the
public were interested in anyone, and always seemed able
to persuade that person to perform under Maskelyne
and Devant's management. Several years earlier, when one of
the periodical revivals of interest in the notorious Tichborne
Claimant Case was capturing the universal fancy, J. N.
engaged Orton, the claimant, to do a disappearing trick
at the Egyptian Hall, where he was greeted with enormous
interest and attracted very large crowds.

It will be remembered that Roger Charles Tichborne,
son of a Hampshire millionaire, was lost at sea, and an
Australian butcher named Orton claimed that he was the
missing heir. A valet of Tichborne's, brother officers of his

former regiment, the family solicitor from Winchester, old tenants on the estates, and even the dead man's mother all believed that the claimant was the true Roger Charles.

But English law decided otherwise after one of the most sensational trials ever held, and troops had to be held in readiness in London when Parliament rejected a motion to refer the case to a Royal Commission. Orton, the claimant, was sent to prison. On his release, he appeared—and disappeared—at the Egyptian Hall, a tribute to my grandfather's flair for showing just what the public wanted. Orton was a great attraction there, particularly to countrymen from Hampshire, who had had a burning personal interest in the case. It is said that there are old villagers even today on the Tichborne estates who have never been convinced that Arthur Orton was an impostor, and still believe that his degradation and imprisonment were the result of a persecution by Jesuit Societies who hoped to gain if the lost heir never came into his fortunes.

After the advent of Mr. Devant, the Maskelyne show went on from strength to strength. In an endeavour to keep fresh novelties before the public, my grandfather began at the time to dabble with Black Magic performances, and study ancient books and musty pamphlets concerning the Black Arts.

On the stage he presented a "Black Magic Well" with which some amazing tricks were performed, and also some shows in which Mephistopheles and members of his fallen fraternity appeared.

Whether the intensive study he made of the Black Arts at this time affected J. N.'s nerves, I cannot say, but he had an experience in the early years of the present century which decided him never to dabble with this ancient magic again, and of which he was very reluctant to speak afterwards.

One morning, working at some apparatus he was

erecting under the stage at the Egyptian Hall, Grandfather noticed a strong smell of burning. Looking up quickly, he saw a small man in black silk clothes standing not far from him, looking on.

This man looked like the actor whom J. N. had engaged for a magical playlet in which the Devil appeared, and who had actually performed the previous two nights on the Egyptian Hall stage. But he certainly had no business there at that time in the morning, nor was it to be expected that he would be in costume and make-up.

When J. N. asked him what he was doing there, he did not reply ; and when my grandfather took a step towards him, he vanished more surprisingly than any magician ever vanished from a stage.

Supposing that the man had chosen this dramatic way of introducing to his notice a new disappearing trick, my grandfather called to him, and eventually, receiving no reply, went behind the stage into his private office, where he expected to find the actor ready with some sort of explanation.

The door of this office, which had been open, was now shut, and J. N. heard movements inside. He strode in, meeting a stench of sulphur, but the place was empty. Also, a pile of books on the Black Arts which had been open on the table were flung hastily about. One of them was missing. It was never found.

The sequel was even more amazing. That morning, still believing that the actor who took the Devil in the playlet had contrived some inexplicable trick on him, J. N. went to his address, only to find that no one of that description had ever stayed there. The man was never seen again, and an understudy had to be hastily rehearsed in the part for that evening's performance.

What was it ? Elaborate practical joke ? Insane terror

at a petty theft ? Or something blacker and more mysterious than either ? The problem has never been solved; but J. N. took Black Art playlets off as soon as he could after that, and would never dabble with witchcraft again.

In 1902, I myself may be said first to have taken the stage, in the part of leading man at my own christening. J. N. was present, of course, but I omitted to ask him how he felt at this great performance.

Three years later, after a long and brilliantly successful tenancy, Maskelynes quitted the Egyptian Hall to move to a theatre of their own—St. George's Hall, in Regent Street. Mr. William Morton, who had been for so long manager and guide to my grandfather and his show, left the concern and branched out on his own, becoming very famous as a theatrical manager, and discovering some of the finest talent that has since adorned the British stage. Mr. Cooke ceased to be an active participant, leaving this department in the capable hands of Mr. Devant. My father, Nevil Maskelyne, took a financial interest in the concern; but over all J. N. ruled supreme, as he had always done, no matter what his nominal position.

He was the type of man who must always rule supreme; through him Maskelynes' Mysteries were conceived and had their being; and his spirit still inspires me today.

CHAPTER VII

Opening at St. George's Hall—Faced with failure—Devant becomes a partner—A wizard curate—I make my bow—Archdeacon Colley offers a £1000 challenge—Into the Courts—"A Side Issue".

TAKING over a West End Theatre is a stupendous undertaking. A very large sum of money is inevitably involved ; and a reputation is put to the test.

It was one thing for Maskelynes' Mysteries to be successful at the Egyptian Hall, on a tenancy renewed over short periods, and quite another matter to take root in London and open a great theatre for no other purpose than the display of magic. It had never been done before ; and there did not lack pessimists and doubters to tell J. N. that he was heading for the Bankruptcy Courts when, in the latter end of 1904, negotiations for St. George's Hall were completed and rehearsals began for the gala performance that was to celebrate the move.

J. N., fearless as ever, decided to do the thing in style. He commissioned David Murray and my father, Nevil Maskelyne, to write and produce a special magic play from Lord Lytton's novel, *The Coming Race*, and a very famous caste, headed by Vera Beringer, was engaged.

As for St. George's Hall, which was at the time in a ruinous condition structurally and marred by a more than doubtful reputation, J. N. almost completely rebuilt it. The stage and its lighting and effects were magnificent, but the auditorium was not reconstructed on quite the same lavish scale.

The floor of the outer vestibule, for instance, was covered with linoleum ; the stone stairs were left bare ; there was no proper bar in the theatre (and in those days it was said that theatres were built around their bars !) ; the cheaper seats were uncomfortable wooden forms, and even the better ones were none too luxurious ; there were no boxes, and the furniture and fittings were almost inclined to shabbiness.

On January 2nd, 1905, the new theatre opened, and a distinguished company of guests and patrons gave a tremendous welcome to the company and producers after the first performance of *The Coming Race*. J. N. prepared for one of the triumphs of his life.

And then, so fickle is public fancy, bookings dwindled almost to vanishing-point within a couple of weeks. The "hoodoo" of St. George's Hall reared its ugly head and menaced my grandfather not only with theatrical failure and an ignominious dismissal back to the provinces, but with the very bankruptcy that the Doubting Thomases among his acquaintances had foretold.

For eight black weeks he kept *The Coming Race* playing to almost empty houses, while he paid its losses out of his own pocket. Two shows a day were given, and the new style of "matinée" performances, of which my grandfather was the originator, attracted a good deal of notice.

Sir Henry Irving, who had been one of the warmest admirers of the new play, came into J. N.'s office one afternoon and asked if there was any objection to his borrowing the idea of matinée performances for his own theatrical ventures. From this beginning the presentation of regular matinées in London sprang.

Towards the end of February it became obvious that *The Coming Race* must be taken off. J. N.'s creditors were pressing him ; like all famous men, he had made many enemies, and these were avidly prophesying his forthcoming ruin; the new theatre was less than half full, even on Saturday evenings.

At this crisis of his career, J. N. remained absolutely undismayed. He recalled Mr. Devant from a successful provincial tour, and behind closed doors had an anxious talk with him. My grandfather had already tried everyone he knew in an endeavour to find backers who would finance him so as to meet the now unceasing demands of his creditors. He had failed in every direction. It was openly rumoured in London that only a matter of days intervened between him and the filing of his bankruptcy petition.

And then the theatrical world was astounded by the announcement that a huge new show was to open immediately at St. George's Hall, and simultaneously a branch theatre was to open in Paris ! Mr. Devant, after a flying visit to the Continent to arrange for the necessary credits, returned to London as a full-fledged partner in the concern, in time to take a leading part in "A Feast of Magic", the new production for St. George's Hall. J. N., his son Nevil, and J. B. Hansard were also to appear.

Tremendous advertising along lines then entirely novel in the theatrical profession titillated London's interest so that the advance bookings for the new show already promised success even before it was opened.

It included some astounding Japanese juggling acts, among which was an absolutely hair-raising knife-throwing trick ; movie-pictures ; a trick in which J. N. vanished while actually being held by members of the audience ; a magical playlet ; and a sensational fire-swallowing act.

The latter looks extraordinary, for in it the performer licks genuinely red-hot pokers, puts flaming balls of tow into his mouth, and submits his tongue to tests with molten metal which would sear the horniest hand.

The secret is simple, and is now very widely known.

The tongue is coated with powdered sugar and soap before the performance, when it becomes perfectly insensible to heat. At the same time, I offer a most serious warning to amateur conjurers who feel inclined to try any such trick in their repertoire. These fire tricks need the most skilful, personal tuition, and endless practice; they are liable to have serious or even fatal results if rashly attempted by novices.

On the opening night of "A Feast of Magic", St. George's Hall was pretty well filled. Next night queues formed long before the show opened, and the theatre was filled to capacity. After that, it was a matter of turning the public away. Straight magic had done what the actor's art had failed to do.

For four months this state of things continued. Then, at the height of its success, J. N. withdrew the show, for he knew the value of leaving off at the psychological moment before receipts began to show any decline, and while the performance was still the talk of the town.

Meanwhile, Mr. Devant had been perfecting one of the most wonderful illusions ever shown on the public stage. This was nothing less than a trick in which he walked up to a woman, in the middle of a fully lighted stage, away from curtains and trap-doors, attempted to embrace her—and, hey presto! she vanished instantly from his arms, in full view of the entire audience.

Mr. Devant himself has since explained the origin of this amazing trick. He says that his wife saw him rise from bed one night, and go through all the actions of the illusion, his eyes being wide open at the time, and then return to bed again without ever having waked up. He was sleep-walking.

Next morning, he tried out the trick, had an apparatus made, and found that it worked perfectly in every detail.

The trick was presented in a most artistic form. The lady in question fluttered on to the stage wearing the make-up of a great moth. Mr. Devant approached her with a candle and she vanished. The illusion was put into a playlet with a mystical setting in the Indian Frontier hills and was one of the biggest successes ever staged.

Meanwhile, the Parisian branch of Maskelyne and Devant Mysteries, as the firm was now called, was registering just as great successes as its London counterpart. The volatile Gaul flocked in his thousands to see the amazing tricks that were presented for his amusement.

There was a rather amusing interlude there just at this time. J. N. had engaged a very clever magician, an English curate who was filling in time while waiting for a living by doing brilliant little magic shows, and this reverend gentleman performed in Paris under a *nom de théatre*.

The Bishop of his diocese happened to be spending a short holiday in the French capital, and was scandalized to see, on a big Maskelyne poster, a photograph which his incredulous eyes told him was of one of his most promising young acolytes.

To convince himself even against his will, the Bishop, complete in gaiters and distinctive top-hat ornamented with the little aerials that marked it out from others of its class, marched solemnly up to the box office of the Parisian theatre, took a single stall, and sat in righteous indignation throughout the performance, during which he doubtless received shocks which afterwards made him offer up special invocations against necromancy.

Later still, our young clerical magician was invited—or commanded—to the Bishop's hotel, where he was solemnly condemned by bell, book and candle for having performed unholy tricks in such an abandoned den of vice as a Parisian variety hall.

There was some talk of his being unfrocked, but the young man, with perfect courtesy, asked why it was so much worse for him to appear on the stage in what was admittedly a perfectly unexceptionable performance and company than for his Bishop to sit and enjoy the whole production from the comfort of the stalls.

The Bishop's reply may be left to the imagination ; but the curate was not unfrocked, and has since risen to the distinction of a Rural Deanery in England, where he is universally loved and admired as well by his flock as his colleagues.

In London, Maskelyne and Devant's was now out of all danger of financial trouble, and was scoring success after success. Many famous magicians applied for the honour of appearing at the new theatre in Langham Place, and some of the applicants, both famous and otherwise, had to be turned away because the company was already so numerous.

Julian Wylie was one of the amateur magicians who applied for a job there. I wonder if he would have made as great an illusionist, had Fate gone his way then, as he has since become a producer. On the whole, I am glad he chose his present path ; I cannot think that any magic, however marvellous, could have recompensed the world for the loss of the present and past glories of "Julian Wylie Productions".

It was about this time that I made my very first bow on the Maskelyne stage. It was not, indeed, so much a bow as what Shakespeare called a "sound off".

I was about three years old at the time, and I had wandered into the wings while a performance was in progress on the St. George's Hall stage. My grandfather was on the stage, in a sketch called *The Hermit of Killarney*, and my father was just about to make his entrance to assist in the piece.

The scene on the stage was that of a rocky cell in the Irish mountains, and some most effective natural phenomena were being reproduced to give the right atmosphere.

It was at this dramatic moment that the old hermit in his meditations, and most of the people in the theatre also, heard my clear, childish treble inquiring : "Daddy, is that Dod's thunder or Grandpa's thunder ?"

The hermit's mouth twitched, the "effects" redoubled to hide a perceptible titter from the audience, and I was withdrawn into a painful obscurity.

As a matter of fact, J. N. was notable for his realistic stage reproductions of thunder, rain and wind. At a time when these things were generally very artificially produced on the legitimate stage, and when clouds, suns and moons were usually painted on wrinkled and dusty backcloths, he and my father were already experimenting with an apparatus which was more or less the forerunner of the "artificial horizon" now used in London's biggest theatres.

In its improved form, this is an expanse of plain white canvas tightly stretched over semi-circular rails behind the stage, like the inside of a cylinder. It acts as a reflector of light ; on it play moving pictures of cloudscapes actually photographed from the sky.

Owing to technical difficulties, J. N. could not perfect this idea, but he managed to evolve some very natural effects with cloud, rain and so on, and gained a good deal of appreciation for them.

In 1906, there arose the first murmurings of a storm that was shortly to break in fury over St. George's Hall. Some correspondence in the *Daily Telegraph* aroused J. N. to write a letter in which he expressed his usual strong views about spiritualism and media.

This brought a reply from a gentleman called Archdeacon Colley, Rector of Stockton, Warwickshire. He publicly challenged J. N. to bring any machinery he wished to Stockton Rectory, and there reproduce certain spiritualistic phenomena. The Archdeacon said that he had deposited £1000 with his bankers, to be paid to J. N. if the latter succeeded in doing what was asked of him.

The chief phenomenon mentioned was to cause a mist to come forth from the side of a man, which mist as it emerged turned into a human figure, able to speak and move about separately from its originator.

For the Archdeacon claimed that a famous spiritualist medium had, in his presence, conjured up such a spirit from his side, and that the spirit talked, wrote letters, walked and ate a baked apple. Who baked the apple, or why the reincarnated dead should prefer this form of diet to a nice dish of banana fritters it seems impossible now to say with any certainty.

It appears that though the spirit ate the apple, the skin and core remained in the mouth *of the medium*, who afterwards mundanely spat them out, whereupon the Archdeacon reverently preserved them as proof to all doubters that the spirit had been real—or at least as real as such extraordinary visitants can be.

To the original challenge from the rural depths of Stockton Rectory, J. N. replied with a certain good-natured levity, pointing out that he himself did not believe in spirits of that sort, and that he wished to be left in his comfortable agnosticism, just as, no doubt, the Archdeacon would like to remain a believer.

I happen to know that my grandfather thought at the time that Archdeacon Colley had been deceived by a certain famous fraudulent medium of the period.

The reverend gentleman would not be appeased, however, and began writing to various newspapers saying that the famous Maskelyne was hedging in face of a public challenge, and that his frequent statements that he could produce any phenomena claimed by spiritualists were merely the wild claims of a self-advertising windbag.

With the intolerance of youth, my father was anxious to take the invitation upon himself, and after some discussion J. N. permitted him and Mr. Devant to reply to the Archdeacon offering to accept the challenge. But the Rector of Stockton was avid for the blood of the Arch-Disbeliever himself.

In the end, the cleric's repeated challenges became such a nuisance that J. N. was forced in his own defence to issue a pamphlet telling what he considered to be the true facts of the whole story. In this pamphlet, he claimed that Mr. Colley was not, in reality, an Archdeacon at all, having had the degree refused him by the then Archbishop of Canterbury, and that, though he commonly wore the hood of an Oxford M.A., he was not entitled to do so.

To this pamphlet, the Rector of Stockton took such strong exception that he sued J. N. for libel. My grandfather's instant reply was a plea of justification and fair comment; and at the same time he reproduced at St. George's Hall the illusion of a spirit form emerging from the side of a man, and then claimed in Court payment of the £1000 offered by the Archdeacon for the performance of this trick.

As a matter of fact, the chief reason why J. N. had been so reluctant hitherto to accept the Archdeacon's challenge was because the latter gentleman could by no means be induced to formulate it in what his opponent thought were reasonable terms—to wit, that he should engage whoever he thought to be the finest medium of the day, that this medium should raise the spirits in a public place before an impartial audience, and that J. N. should then endeavour to reproduce the tricks exact in every detail.

The Archdeacon, while obviously wroth, preferred to

adhere to the very much vaguer terms of his original challenge.

The case was tried before Mr. Justice Ridley and a Special Jury in the King's Bench Division, and created a tremendous sensation. Before they could decide the question as to whether J. N. had earned his £1000, the jury had to go to St. George's Hall to see a performance of the trick in question, which had been aptly named "The Side Issue".

In it, J. N. and his assistant, both clad in long black frock-coats and semi-clerical "dog-collars," stood in the centre of the stage, well away from curtains, trap-doors and so on, and with only a couple of ordinary cane chairs as "properties". The assistant "hypnotized" J. N., made magical passes over him, muttered mystic spells, and J. N. rose to his full height, his eyes shut and a rapt expression on his face.

At this moment, usually to the accompaniment of exclamations of horror and astonishment from the audience, a white mist began to issue from his left side.. This mist thickened till it formed a hand, growing from his side. The hand was followed by an arm ; gradually, there materialized a golden-haired spirit form.

She floated forth from his side horizontally, while J. N. himself stood with shut eyes and white face, apparently in a trance. The spirit then turned her feet to the ground, spoke to the audience in a clear and intelligent way, ate a baked apple if particularly desired to do so, and then, at a sudden pass from the "medium", vanished from before the audience's very eyes, while J. N. uttered a cry, opened his eyes and appeared to emerge from a dream.

The thing was an extraordinarily dramatic and realistic illusion, and the Press and onlookers universally agreed that it fulfilled every detail of Archdeacon Colley's challenge.

What the jury thought could not, of course, be immediately disclosed, but they looked very impressed.

I remember, as a very small boy, watching this illusion from the wings of the theatre, and greeting my aunt (the golden-haired spirit form) as she vanished from human ken and materialized again by my side. I also remember her pointing out the jury to me, as they sat solemnly looking on from the front row of the stalls.

The case returned to the Courts. Mr. Colley agreed that he had known the medium, and admitted that once he had raised "Samuel" from the vasty deeps, and that the Prophet had wrecked the room and behaved "like Hell let loose". This has always seemed to me to be rather a slur on Samuel, but we will let it pass.

As to the alleged libel, Mr. Justice Ridley said in summing up that "the words that the plaintiff was not an archdeacon and never had been an archdeacon were statements of fact", and that "the rest of the pamphlet was not libellous".

As to the counter-claim by J. N. for the £1000 offered by Mr. Colley for the reproduction of the spirit-raising manifestation, it appeared that, though the ghost appeared perfectly satisfactorily, the claim failed on a technical point because the apparition had not returned into J. N.'s side the way it had come, but had suddenly vanished while still some distance from him.

My grandfather was then adjudged by the jury to have libelled Mr. Colley, and to have failed to earn the £1000 offered ! Damages of £75 were given against him in respect of the libel, and he had to pay the very high costs of the long-drawn-out case.

Of course, the matter of returning my aunt apparently into his side was just as simple as her emergence had been. In fact, had Mr. Colley stated exactly what he wished done when he offered his challenge there seems very little room to doubt that he would have lost his £1000.

J. N. was a marvellous man. Far from being downcast at losing the case, he billed "The Side Issue" all over London.

People from the length and breadth of England, whose interest had been excited by reading the long reports that had appeared of the case, came crowding to St. George's Hall, and "The Side Issue" proved to be the biggest draw Maskelynes had ever known. It ran before packed and deliriously delighted audiences for nearly a year.

CHAPTER VIII

The Magic Circle—A dead hand plays dominoes—Spies in St. George's
Hall—Turning over "A New Page"—The Indian Rope Trick—
A magician in the Thames—My first Command Performance—
Ancient temple magic.

IT was about this time—to be exact, I believe at the end of
1905—that the Maigc Circle was formed, under the Presi-
dency of my grandfather.

This association, which has since gathered into its
membership all the most famous magicians of the Eastern
and Western world, was formed largely to prevent the
secrets of magic from being publicly exposed, and also as
far as possible to protect the presentation of new magical
effects in favour of the inventor.

It will easily be seen how difficult this latter concern
might be. You can patent apparatus to produce an illusion,
but you cannot patent the illusion. Once a skilful magician
has seen an illusion worked on the stage, he can usually,
in the case of a trick of average intricacy, deduce how it is
done. There are notable exceptions, of course.

For instance, J. N.'s Box Trick defied imitation so successfully that for many years he offered £1000 to anyone
who could reproduce it. In the invention of automata, too,
he was unequalled, and Zoe, Psycho, Labial and the rest
have never been successfully copied to this day. Nor have
some of the Maskelyne vanishing tricks.

But J. N. was admittedly the greatest magician of his
time, if not the greatest ever known in the world's history.
Others might suffer from imitation where he went free.

THE STORY OF MASKELYNES   101

The Magic Circle, therefore, had a definite work to do, and still performs that work today.

It holds an annual meeting, at which new members are admitted, new tricks shown, and the progress of world magic during the past twelve months discussed. Incidentally, admission is jealously guarded, and only superlative magicians of unexceptionable character can be accepted; it is probably more difficult to enter the Magic Circle than to obtain a commission in a crack regiment.

This is a necessary precaution. Two or three times during my grandfather's life we discovered spies at St. George's Hall intent on trying to steal the secrets of our finest illusions.

On only one occasion did they succeed. Usually a polite note was passed to them, as they sat in the stalls, asking them to leave the theatre—a request that was never ignored.

But once, shortly after the Magic Circle had been founded, one of our magicians at St. George's Hall was on the stage with an assistant. He muttered a mystic incantation, made some magical passes, and the assistant should have vanished from before the very eyes of the audience.

At the critical moment, however, someone in the stalls uttered a sudden sharp scream, and at the same time a scene-shifter in the wings, who had been engaged temporarily that day in place of another man who was ill, shone a bright electric torch into the eyes of the magician.

The result was that the wizard vanished, and the assistant stayed where she was. What was more to the point, the "works" of the trick were discovered. The following evening, the identical trick was being performed in another London theatre.

If this sort of thing were to happen often, the finest illusionists would be put out of work while their tricks were presented with much financial success by thieving rivals.

Therefore the Magic Circle makes very sure, before it closes its doors for one of its annual conferences, that no spy has concealed himself within the precincts, and that every member present is a man of honour and discretion.

Perhaps the most astonishing new trick ever exhibited to the members of the Magic Circle was devised by that master magician, Mr. Devant, and displayed at the annual meeting in 1909.

He passed round among the company a glass case in which reposed a withered yellow hand. This hand had belonged to a Japanese philosopher of the sixteenth century, and had been preserved because of certain magical properties which the owner was said to have passed into it on his death.

At the Magic Circle meeting four hundred years later the hand was removed from the case and placed on a small trolley, hand and trolley being then returned to the inside of the closed case, in which a number of dominoes had first been scattered.

Three independent members of the audience then hid behind a screen, and a weird game of dominoes commenced. The three magicians played their best, but the hand, running to and fro on its trolley without any human agency and picking up in its withered fingers its own selection of dominoes, won each game. Mr. Devant said that it had never been known to lose.

By this time, my father, Nevil Maskelyne, was President of the Circle. He was present on this occasion, other distinguished guests being Herr Stackemann, Mr. Carl Hertz, Mr. Jack Merlin, Dr. Wilmar, Mr. Herbert Collings, and, of course, Mr. Devant himself. Doubtless some of them will remember the occasion still.

Mr. Devant was by this time making a world-wide reputation as a master illusionist. He had recently invented a trick which he entitled "The New Page", and which created a great sensation when it was presented at St. George's Hall. I think it one of the cleverest things of its kind ever staged.

A box was carried in pieces on to the stage, and there put together after each piece had been held up for examination by the audience. When erected, it was found to be a small coffin, exactly big enough to fit one of the diminutive page-boys of the theatre. The coffin was stood on end; the page squeezed into it, and was there securely strapped to an iron bar running the full length of the inside of the coffin. The lid was then screwed on, when the coffin rose slowly of its own accord, and remained suspended in mid-air about six feet from the stage.

Mr. Devant then took a doll in his hand, and explained to the audience that whatever he did with the doll, the page-boy must also do, because he was under a sympathetic spell with the little figure.

With a sudden dramatic motion, the doll was then turned upside down. The coffin-lid was swiftly unscrewed—and the page-boy was also found to be upside down, though still strapped to the iron bar as firmly as ever. It was quite obviously impossible for the boy, or the bar, to move inside the closed coffin. How was it done? I dare say the answer would surprise you!

The one trick that Maskelynes admitted that they could *not* perform was the Indian Rope Trick. In fact, my grandfather issued a challenge, which was broadcast not only all over Europe and America, but throughout the length and breadth of India, that he would pay £10,000 down, or £1000 down and a salary of £250 a week, to any fakir who could do this trick to his satisfaction, and show him how to do it himself.

So many incorrect versions of the Indian Rope Trick

have been printed that I should perhaps outline this illusion in the original form of the legend.

The fakir must perform the trick in an open field, away from trees or any other obstacles. He must produce a rope, let it be examined by an independent audience who must pass it as genuine, and then he must throw the rope about fifteen feet in the air, where it should remain vertical and rigid, though without any visible means of support.

A boy must then climb the rope to its top, and vanish. The fakir follows with a knife in his teeth, and slashes about in the air at the top, whereupon limbs, a head, and pieces of flesh cut from the boy's body fall to the ground.

Finally, the fakir descends the rope, pulls it down and coils it up, throws the limbs and pieces of body into a bag, places the bag in a box which has previously been examined by the audience—and within a minute the box opens and the boy jumps out, alive and whole.

This trick has never been performed.

I am well aware that hundreds of travellers claim to have seen it. I am also aware that India was searched from end to end, during the occasion of the late King George's visit there in 1902, when he was Prince of Wales, and that no one could find a fakir who could perform the trick before him.

I believe the same thing happened during the Duke of Windsor's visit to India.

This trick must not be confounded with a similar one in which the performer places a long bamboo pole on the ground and a boy climbs to the top of it, though the pole has no apparent means of support.

I myself can get farther than that. I can make a *rope* stand up rigid, but I cannot—at least not in an open field— make a boy disappear from the top of it while all eyes watch him.

I can apparently cut a boy to bits, throw down his mutilated remains, throw them in a bag, and reincarnate him whole within a minute, but for this I need a stage. I cannot do it all in an open field, as the fakirs claim to be able to do.

But I have no objection to repeating, on my own account, the challenge originally issued by my grandfather, and repeated later by my father. That challenge has never been answered. It never will be.

The illusionist's business is so far like life that "the best-laid plans . . . oft gang agley". I remember an occasion at Maskelynes' Theatre when a disappearing trick went very wrong indeed.

A magician we had engaged there to fill a gap caused by illness had apparently looked upon the bottle when it was red—and left it plain glass-coloured! Anyway, he walked on to the stage with a donkey which he meant to vanish, trod on the trap-door and vanished himself, leaving the donkey looking rather pleased.

My father walked on, improvised a few words of banter on the difficulty of "vanishing" both a donkey and its driver —and the donkey followed its master. No one realized that anything had gone wrong with the trick.

Once an illusion nearly ended fatally. It was on the occasion of a big outdoor display of magic at a Teddington garden party, attended by my father and some of his cleverest magicians. Many famous people were present to watch the illusions.

The most spectacular trick of the day was one in which a clever English illusionist was to be shut inside an iron cistern, riveted in there by professional riveters not connected with Maskelynes, and then the cistern with the man inside was to be flung bodily into the Thames.

The thing hit the water with a terrific plop, and sank

instantly, amid gasps from the fashionably dressed audience. The waves created by the disturbance subsided into agitated ripples—but still no magician appeared.

No one in the audience except my father and myself realized that the illusionist was long overdue at the surface. Had something gone wrong ? If so, then the show looked like ending in a fatality, for there would be a poor chance of escape for a magician on the Thames bottom if anything faulty occurred in "the works".

And then, to our extraordinary relief, the performer's head broke the surface of the water, and he swam slowly and painfully to shore, amid tremendous applause. As soon as possible, he was taken aside, and the explanation of his long imprisonment under the Thames was explained.

Something *had* gone wrong. Only the consummate nerve and skill of the young magician had saved his life and our reputation, and prevented that sunny afternoon's amusement from being turned into a ghastly tragedy.

It was in July, 1912, that I gave my first Royal Command Performance. I was then nine years old ; as you rightly surmise, therefore, I was not actually named on the list of artistes submitted to Buckingham Palace for His Majesty's approval. But I appeared all the same when the great day came.

The show was to be given at the Palace Theatre, and was the first variety performance by Royal Command before King George V. What a state of excitement I was in when I learned that I was to play my small part on the chosen evening !

The whole theatre was in a turmoil. Over a million bunches of roses were used to decorate it in honour of the Royal visit. In fact, so powerful was the scent from these roses that several people fainted while the Command Performance was actually in progress, and it was learned from that night that artificial roses were advisable in the future. I believe that artificial flowers have usually been used, except in the Royal Box, at gala performances since that date.

The theatre, however, looked indescribably beautiful, and I ran several times to the little peep-hole in the curtain to watch the auditorium filling up with a fashionable throng. Finally, when every seat was taken and people were standing in large numbers at the back, the National Anthem was played, and the curtain rose on the first turn of the show.

Never since has such a collection of variety talent been brought together under one roof. Barclay Gammon, of St. George's Hall fame, was there; Chirgwin, the White-eyed Kaffir; Fanny Fields, in her Dutch clogs; Cinque-valli, the human billiard-table; Harry Tate; Vesta Tilley; Little Tich; Clarice Mayne; George Robey, complete with eyebrows and umbrella; Cissie Loftus; Harry Lauder, grasping a curly stick; Anna Pavlova, then glad of the chance of such an appearance on the variety stage; and Mr. David Devant.

My excitement rose to a climax as the time for Mr. Devant's turn approached. For the time being, I was his assistant, together with his little daughter, Vida.

The preceding turn ended, amid vociferous clapping; the audience waited expectantly, probably hoping that the magician would make an appropriate entrance by material-izing suddenly in the centre of the stage; Mr. Devant walked on, and Vida and I held hands in the wings, awaiting our cue.

Finally, after another minute or two of intolerable suspense, our time came. We walked on together; and speaking for myself, I instantly forgot all about the trick I had to help to perform.

I simply stared up at the Royal Box, where I could see several ladies and gentlemen sitting. I stared again with all the frank unembarrassment of childhood, and then I knitted my brows in a frown.

"Where are the King and Queen?" I whispered to Mr. Devant, who was preparing his trick.

"In the Royal Box," he answered, from the corner of his mouth, and added a warning, "Ssh!"

But nothing could make me *Ssh* now.

"Well, where are their crowns?" I asked in woeful disappointment.

I had been so certain they would be wearing crowns and robes—it seemed to me that Kings and Queens were not real without these appurtenances, and probably never parted from them for a moment, night or day! In my sorrow, I must have raised my voice more than I realized. At any rate, I saw the Queen smile suddenly at me.

I must have been very red as I prepared to help Mr. Devant with the trick, which was an egg illusion that needed deft handling. Also, I was so self-conscious at the effect of my unintentional raising of the voice that I nearly swallowed an egg.

All the same, the King and Queen gave Vida and myself a special clap as we left the stage, and then I felt more thrilled than ever I had done in my life before. Even the absence of the crowns didn't seem to matter then.

So pleased were Their Majesties with Mr. Devant's magic that they specially asked for his name to be included the following year in a variety display to be given in their presence at Knowsley Hall, on the occasion of Lord Derby's heir's coming-of-age party.

At about the same time, St. George's Hall gained further laurels when Mr. Devant was asked to give a magic performance at the opening of the theatre in the new and wonderful Atlantic liner *Aquitania*. I believe she was the very first ship to be fitted with a full-sized theatre, and the

opening night was an occasion of almost national import-
ance. Mr. Devant scored his usual great success, and
invented a new vanishing illusion specially for the occasion.

This illusion was particularly interesting because it was
originally based on a trick performed in Ancient Egypt in
3766 B.C. Mr. Devant found a record of this trick on the
translation of a papyrus in the British Museum, and puzzled
out the method the ancient necromancers had used to perform it. It proved a very effective illusion indeed, and was
subsequently featured at St. George's Hall.

As a matter of fact, the art of magic was perfected to a
marvellous degree in Ancient Egypt. There seems little
room to doubt that those wizards of Pharaoh who tried
unsuccessfully to oppose Moses and Aaron were masters of
magic in their own degree.

We know from contemporary records that the Ancients
performed all sorts of illusions in their temples for the
mystification of the simple worshippers. For instance, there
was a famous temple at Thebes where a trumpet sounded
when the door of a shrine was timidly pushed open by a
worshipper entering to bring offerings. The walls were too
narrow to accommodate any human being, yet the invisible
horns of elfland sounded, doubtless to the great financial
benefit of the local priesthood.

This trick was worked as follows. When the doors
were pushed open, a system of pulleys, cords and rods
pushed into a vessel of water a ball to the upper part of
which a trumpet was fixed. The whole was enclosed in a
sealed cylinder. When the ball entered the water, the air
above was compressed and forced through the trumpet,
giving forth sounds that would have been sufficiently eerie
on a dark night in the midst of a mysterious temple.

Many of the tricks used by the Ancients for Trials by

Ordeal have recently come under the scrutiny of modern magicians, and have been found capable of very simple solutions.

I have already explained the secret of the handling or even touching with the tongue of red-hot irons, and the "swallowing" of fire. On the site of a Greek temple at Athens, excavators a few years ago discovered a magic pitcher which was famous in Greek legend in trials for witchcraft.

This pitcher was perforated with innumerable holes all round its upper half. The priests half-filled the pitcher, passed it to the suspected necromancer, and asked him to drink from it. If he succeeded in doing so, he was innocent ; if not, they burned him alive.

If the unfortunate man tilted the pitcher to bring the water to his lips, it poured out of the holes in the upper half of the vessel, and not a taste reached his mouth. Then one of the priests would take the pitcher and with grave and deliberate enjoyment drink its contents to the dregs without spilling a drop. At which, of course, the concourse roared approbation, and stacked up the faggots that were to form the funeral pyre of the miserable wretch who had failed in the ordeal.

The explanation is simple in the extreme. The handle of the pitcher was hollow, and channels led from the top of the handle inside the rim to the spout. By exerting suction on the spout, the liquid could be drawn up the handle and into the mouth without ever passing the holes in the sides of the pitcher.

Another illusion which gained great kudos for its demonstrators among the Greek temple virgins, and which offered a convenient way of getting rid of unwanted people, was the ordeal in which a girl apparently had a sword passed through her stomach, the end projecting from her back, yet suffered no wound. When the victim was stabbed similarly with the same sword, death resulted.

This trick was very simply performed, and is still in use on the stage to this day, so that I cannot explain its workings without breaking the unwritten laws of magic. But I could perform it upon any of my assistants, employing a real sword, not one whose blade telescopes.

Most famous of all the tricks of ancient temple magic was the Delphic oracle, which was simply worked by means of an ordinary speaking-tube.

Another common ordeal was to make a victim walk on red-hot irons, or on broken glass. In the case of the irons, the priest who demonstrated the possibility of performing the act with the god's approval and without damage anointed his feet with sugar and fat as in the fire-eating trick.

If broken glass were chosen for the ordeal, two trays were prepared, each apparently containing identical broken glass. But in the priest's tray, each piece of the glass in the middle was filed fairly smooth at the edges, though that which ornamented the outer parts of the tray nearest the congregation was genuine sharp-edged stuff. However, the priest walked carefully in the middle only.

In addition, feet were usually prepared by preliminary soaking in strong alum water, and rosin in powdered form was rubbed well into them afterwards. Thus the priest once more triumphantly demonstrated how valuable it was to have a pure heart, while the victim, after having had his feet cut to bits on the sharper glass of his tray, was usually sacrificed in some peculiarly unpleasant manner to appease the spirits he had angered.

The only genuine trick used by the Ancients in their temples was sword-swallowing, and this, it is significant to note, was never permitted as an ordeal.

It is about the most interesting bit of magic in the whole of the legendary collection, because it is actually and really sword-swallowing. There is no telescopic blade or any hocus-pocus like that.

The art of the thing lies simply in this, that the throat of a human being, if constantly rubbed and pressed on the inside, becomes so calloused that it will swallow almost anything, without the slightest sensation of disgust, though a normal throat will "invert" merely at the touch of a spoon or a finger.

Once the sword-swallower has trained his throat to be insensible to the touch of steel, however, all he has to do is to throw back his head, so that his throat and internal orifices are in a straight line, put the point of the sword in his mouth, tap the hilt—and the blade slides down into his stomach, where the point may be felt by manual pressure on the outside of the belly.

Medical men will confirm that there is a space all the way down, and that nothing but nausea need prevent anyone from performing this amazing trick.

Indeed, medicine has to acknowledge a great debt to the sword-swallowing profession. For in 1777 a doctor of the name of Stevens conducted the first practical studies ever carried out concerning human gastric juices by the aid of one of the conjuring fraternity.

He persuaded his man to swallow some small steel capsules, filled with meat, the capsules being drilled with holes to permit the juices to attack the meat. After a set number of hours, the swallower disgorged them again, and the doctor noted the effects of the stomach action on the meat.

These experiments were continued on various occasions, since the swallower possessed the rare faculty (sometimes still found among magicians of this sort) of returning stomach contents by a simple movement of the digestive muscles, without inconvenience to himself.

From similar experiments it was discovered how to introduce a small electric light into the stomach—a method much used by modern doctors and surgeons nowadays; and also how to introduce tubes down the throat into the stomach so as to carry food there direct, or to wash out the stomach when desired.

Although all this is old knowledge now to doctors, the general public today is just as much impressed as ever when it sees sword-swallowing carried out cleverly; just as astonished, in fact, as the Ancients undoubtedly were when sword-swallowing priests claimed to be performing magic by the direct assistance of the gods themselves.

Certainly it would be as impossible for an uninitiated modern to swallow a sword as it was for those poor pagans who, failing in other rituals, were thereupon done to death with much rejoicing by those who had formerly marked them down for extinction because they happened to be in somebody's way.

Although I myself am a professional magician, and should have stood a very good chance, I suppose, in the old days of becoming a High Priest, I am much more satisfied to belong to this quieter era. A conjurer's life is not all roses nowadays; but at least one has a fair chance to acquire the tricks of the trade without being dragged off to the temple of a rival practitioner and submitted to a swindling ordeal inevitably ending in one's own discomfiture and death and the great glorification of one's rival.

CHAPTER IX

Slow-motion photography experiments—Photographing artillery shells in flight—Nearly a tragedy—Maskelynes help the Admiralty during the war—Magicians help Lawrence of Arabia—My first ghost.

AFTER an extraordinarily busy and eventful life, my grandfather began to loose the reins of authority at St. George's Hall. Having piloted the new venture past doubts, dangers and difficulties into prosperous seas, he handed over the tiller into Mr. Devant's capable hands. At the same time, though he was just as interested as ever in inventions, both of his own and other people's, he slackened his efforts in this direction, and my father, Nevil Maskelyne, carried on the family tradition.

I have said that J. N. experimented with early movie cameras, and gave movie shows at the Theatre of Mysteries long before the earliest cinematograph companies had formed in America. From this, the next step was towards slow-motion photography.

For many years my father experimented with cameras intended to produce movies that would enable the eye to follow the movements of birds' wings in flight. He was academically interested in the various problems of aviation, then in its infancy at Hendon and elsewhere, and he made various researches into the possibility of building a machine whose wings would beat like a bird's or a bee's, attaining if possible the same relative speed and climbing-power in relation to weight that the latter insect possesses.

By photographing birds with slow-motion cameras he tried to tackle the question of human flight unaided by mechanical power. His first idea was the fitting of wings on the arms and legs of the flyer, as he held a theory that flight could be accomplished in this way if only the would-be aeronaut practised enough. Swimming—indeed, even walking—cannot be mastered at the first or second attempt; he thought flying with wings on arms and legs would similarly yield to continued effort, directed by a thorough knowledge of the movements of birds in flight.

Later, he turned to the possibility of building gliders, and actually constructed models capable of sustained flight if started by fast towing, in just the same way that gliders work today. His models, I remember, were built on very similar lines to the modern German "Kondor" glider, which has attained a gliding height record of some 20,000 feet.

It was during these experiments, with their corollary work upon slow-motion photography of birds in flight, that my father was asked to conduct certain research work for the War Office at the artillery station at Shoeburyness. An argument had developed in distinguished quarters in the Army about the flight of shells from big guns, and this, it was suggested, might be settled by photographing shells in flight.

The point at issue was whether shells travelled nose-forward all the time, or whether they rolled over and over so that sometimes the side and sometimes the butt of the shell was towards the enemy. It became essential, in connection with the number of shells that failed to explode properly when fired on to sandy ground, to discover whether these shells landed nose-first, or whether they could fall broadside on to the sand, and so lose some of their effectiveness.

I accompanied my father to Shoeburyness, and we took a number of big and rather clumsy cameras, over whose safety he watched jealously throughout the journey. At

H

the camp, we were received pleasantly by officers and men, and I soon made friends with the good-natured artillery privates who were detailed to serve the guns whose shells had to be photographed.

They talked freely before me, as I was quite small at the time, and I remember they were very mirthful about the chance of photographing a big shell once it had been fired. One must remember that slow-motion photography was quite unheard of by the general public in those pre-war days, and far less was known even about moving pictures than we now know about television.

On the morning when the experiment was to be made, I went out with Father to the corner of the field he had selected as a suitable place in which to set up his camera. Getting tired of watching him fitting the parts together, I wandered off along the hedge towards the big gun, round which a group of artillerymen were already moving.

I loitered along the hedge, looking for birds' nests, and eventually arrived within a few yards of the gun. Then, seeing a man I knew on the far side of it, I strolled out directly across the line in which it was pointing.

At the same time I heard an officer counting—"EIGHT—NINE—*WAIT, MEN, WAIT !*"

He had glanced up and seen me out of the corner of his eye ; and I was told afterwards that only the sheerest luck had saved me from being blown to bits by walking across in front of the gun as it was fired. The officer held a watch in his hand, and was just about to give the command to fire the shell for which my father was waiting.

At the time, though from the shocked faces of my friends round the gun and the unparliamentary word or two addressed to me by the officer I understood that something had gone wrong, I did not realize how near I had been to departing suddenly from this life.

I stayed and watched the gun fired and then fired again two or three times. Finally, a distant whistle from my father told that he had obtained the pictures he wanted.

Then we left the smoking 60-pounder gun, and at my urgent request went along to the place where the shells had landed. The officer in charge rather cynically suggested that I might like to keep, as a memento, the one that had nearly ended my young life, and the artillery men dug it out for me.

It was sunk twenty-eight feet deep in the ground. When it was finally retrieved, and I stood, hands in pockets, staring down into the crater from which it had been dug, I got a clearer idea of what I had escaped when the gun went off. I still have that 60-pound shell in my drawing-room today, and often tell my own children its story as they pat its glossy black sides.

It only remains to add that the photography was perfectly successful, and proved beyond any doubt that shells travel nose-forward, with a slight wobble, throughout their course.

This was by no means the only occasion on which Maskelynes came to the assistance of the Government. I have already told how J. N. conducted innumerable experiments with war balloons, filling them more quickly than any rival, and how the results of his work proved invaluable to the Army during the South African War. I have also told the story of Douglas Beaufort, Maskelyne magician, and his political trip to Morocco.

But perhaps the most interesting of all these semi-official tasks was undertaken by my father during the European War.

Our theatre, at the time, was filled with the khaki and blue of soldiers and sailors home on leave, and our magic shows and playlets were adapted to suit the spirit of the times. But we were soon to come into closer contact with hostilities.

One morning my father found beside his plate at the breakfast table an official-looking letter bearing the stamp of the Admiralty and marked "Highly Confidential". This letter explained how it had become necessary, for certain reasons connected with His Majesty's Navy, to make investigations into methods used to protect the skin against fire, and asked Father to call at the Admiralty at a given date and time.

In due course he kept the appointment, and was met by some very important members of the Admiralty. These explained to him that at the Battle of Jutland, which had then recently taken place, numbers of British gunners had been badly burned by the back-flash from the big naval guns during the conflict with the German ships.

It appeared that the guns were served by crews who, in battle, had a fifteen-minute spell of duty, and then about the same period of rest while another team took on the working of the great sixteen-inch weapons.

But it was discovered at Jutland that the gun-teams were so badly burned, in some cases, after fifteen minutes at a gun, that they could not carry on again after their spell of rest. So it happened that, with the German Fleet more or less at our mercy, we were unable to achieve the complete victory which should have rewarded Earl Jellicoe's tactics.

This is the more interesting because so many theories have been advanced for our incomplete victory at Jutland. Admiral after Admiral on the German side has marvelled that their Fleet was allowed to escape, after being manœuvred into a hopeless position. The secret, as far as I can make out, was simply this, that our gunners, staggering back half-blinded and smoke-blackened from the guns, as the weapons slid like striking snakes to and fro on their mountings, could not force their scorching flesh to lay and fire the guns adequately; and so what was perhaps an opportunity to end the war in half the time it subsequently took was wasted.

Someone with initiative at the Admiralty, unafraid to depart from tradition after this disaster, approached my father and asked him for the Maskelyne secret of playing with fire.

It was, of course, well known that our magicians frequently appeared to eat fire on the stage, thrust their hands into leaping flames, licked red-hot pokers, and put burning tow in their mouths. It was obvious that some secret preparation must be used to render the skin insensitive to heat.

If this preparation could be served out to the gunners of the Grand Fleet, then they would be able to serve their guns till the ships belched forth the very fires of Hell, and still remain unhurt. And so, as I say, there came a request from the Admiralty seeking the secret of our fire-immunity.

The formula we use is one whose details have never been divulged to the world, so I cannot publish it now.

I have already mentioned, in an earlier chapter, a simple formula for fire-protection, but I would again emphasize that I do not advise amateurs to attempt these dangerous tricks without most careful practice and preparation. .

When my father told our secret formula to the Admiralty chemists, they tested it thoroughly and were astounded at its efficacy. It was finally served out to the naval gunners. When these men had pasted up their hands and faces with the preparation, they found they could fire the great guns incredibly quickly, undamaged either by the flames from the breech or the almost red-hot metal itself.

That was one of the ways in which magic helped

England during the dark hours of the war. There were other ways, too, though I am only at liberty to mention one other that came within my knowledge at the time.

Colonel Lawrence—"Lawrence of Arabia"—sent a request to the Government here, at the most critical period of his desert campaign, asking for magicians to be sent out to travel among the tribes on the borders of the Mediterranean and Red Sea, to pose as wandering native Holy Men, perform big magic, gain a reputation for prophecy and power—and prophesy the defeat of the Turks.

He specified that the magicians, if it were humanly possible, should be Arabs themselves, and that in no case should anyone be sent who was not entirely familiar with the habits and customs and the very thoughts of the natives among whom they were to move. It was obvious, of course, that widespread disastrous results would follow the detection and exposure of these "Holy Men" as impostors doing propaganda work for England !

Five magicians were sent out, three of them Arabs, one a Frenchman who had spent a large part of his life in Arabia, and one an Englishman whom the latter trained till he was letter-perfect in his part.

The Frenchman and one of the Arabs disappeared. The desert swallowed them up. No one knows, even today, whether they were detected and tortured to death, or whether they lost their way in the shifting sands and died horribly of thirst beside their dead riding-camels, or whether they turned native after the war and stayed in the East. They joined the silent army of the "Missing".

The other three carried out their work with a success probably hardly foreseen even by Lawrence himself. Moving to and fro over the sand-hills, gaining great reputations, refusing all rewards, ascetic Marabouts whose least word was gathered up and treasured, they foretold the defeat of Turkey, and gained credence for this greater fact by industriously prophesying all sorts and varieties of minor military affairs, which invariably happened exactly "according to Cocker". The explanation, of course, was that Lawrence and his Intelligence Department saw to it that the "Holy Men" got news in advance of everything that was going to happen.

Gradually the Turks found their native allies deserting them. Trouble prophesied for certain waverers who persisted in supporting the Turkish Armies always came down in the end on the waverers' devoted heads—Allah (or Lawrence) saw to that. Eventually, since it grew so painfully clear that the "Holy Men" were right, and that Allah fought on the side of the Allies, the Turks lost all their native support, and Lawrence gained what they lost.

We have lost touch with the two Arab Secret Service magicians since the war, but the Englishman is now a great authority on bees, and has a prosperous little bee-farm in Gloucestershire. Native memories are long, and he will not allow his name to be published, but one or two of his intimate acquaintances in the local Beekeepers' Association can verify my story with more details than I have given here; for the gentleman in question becomes quite loquacious about his desert adventures on the evenings when some of his exhibits have gained prizes in local honey shows.

Let me return to my schoolboy memories of my father. One of the most vivid to me, which also took place during the war, though it had nothing to do with the struggle, concerns also my first acquaintance with ghosts.

I was sitting in my father's dressing-room one evening during a show at St. George's Hall, when a message arrived for Father, who had just come off the stage, and was removing his make-up there before a mirror. Presently a girl of about twenty was shown in.

She had seen the show, including a very spectacular "ghost-raising" trick, in which Father first made a mist appear on the stage, and from it materialized a white phantom which spoke, moaned, and generally behaved as all good phantoms do.

The girl, who was in a pathetic state of earnestness, wanted to know whether, as we could raise ghosts, we could also lay them.

It seemed that she was the daughter of a small landowner in Kent. The old man, always rather prone to superstition, had for the past two years been almost driven mad by a ghost which haunted the wood behind his house. After seeing this apparition at close quarters on two or three occasions, he had suffered a nervous breakdown, and was now very ill.

A climax had been put to the affair when the daughter herself saw the ghost, as she returned one evening from the village. It "jumped at her", gliding through the air, and she described it as a "white, shapeless figure that moaned". Being only very young myself at the time, the phrase sank into my mind.

My father asked a number of questions, and then, to my amazement, promised to come down and "lay the ghost". The girl went away implicitly believing in his power to do so, and greatly comforted. I naturally bombarded him with inquiries, but he preserved a grim silence.

"You shall come with me and see it all in good time," he said finally. I was delighted, but must confess to certain tremors.

It was just after Christmas that the girl had called on my father, and he chose New Year's Eve as the time when he would endeavour to tackle the apparition, presumably because that is a famous time for ghosts to "walk".

On New Year's Eve, therefore, we arrived at a little

Kentish station, and travelled thence, by means of a pony-trap, to the village we sought, which was about three miles from Biddenden. Dismissing the trap, we proceeded on foot into the haunted wood.

Father had arranged with the girl who told us the story to walk through the wood, past the haunted glade, at about ten o'clock. She was also—and he was insistent on this—to let the servants at home know of her intention.

At about a quarter to ten Father and I took up a position in a thick clump of hazels just beside the path, commanding a good view of that section where the ghost had always previously appeared. Father carried in the crook of his arm a sporting-gun loaded with specially prepared cartridges filled with saltpetre instead of shot.

The darkness in the wood was intense, and it was so cold that it felt as if thorns were thrust under one's finger- and toe-nails. Yet Father insisted that we both crouched motionless in our places, watching the faintly illumined patches of moonlight on the path.

As the silence grew, it became filled with little wood-land noises of the night—flittering of leaves, tiny sighs, ghostly movements and the echoes of elvish chattering. Suddenly, without warning, a great white form sailed over us, soundlessly, and I realized that a hunting owl had gone by, seeking food. It cried mournfully a second later, like the plaint of a lost soul.

From far away in the stillness, sounding little and musical like the horns of elfland, I heard the village clock strike ten.

As if the sound had rung up the curtain on some wood-land drama, there became evident to the ear a distant occasional crackle, which rapidly grew into the sound of light footsteps among the leaves far along the path. Then the girl who had brought us here came into view, walking quickly, with rapid, nervous turns of the head to right and left.

At the same moment several things happened. I saw Father throw up his gun and heard the deafening crash of it bursting the night silence. The blaze of the explosion momentarily dazzled my eyes, but, just before, I had seen a white, impalpable monster, shapeless, but dreadfully resembling a corpse in grave-clothes, sweep along the path, some three or four feet from the ground, in a tremendous inhuman leap towards the shrinking girl ahead. Simultaneously with the report of the gun there rose a sharp, horrible scream, and the apparition vanished.

Father ran to the girl, who was half-fainting, ahead of us. She was trembling all over when I arrived, but I could hear her still murmuring: "Did you see it? Oh, did you see it?"

Her courageous action in venturing into the haunted wood that night, however, helped to lay the Biddenden ghost for ever.

Next day, Father went along to the local doctor, and I was allowed to accompany him.

"Have you any patients this morning who are suffering from swollen legs?" Father asked.

"Swollen legs! Good heavens, how do *you* know anything about it, sir?" asked the doctor apoplectically. "Swollen legs! Why, Blank, up at the Farm, has got legs like pillow-cases. He says he shot himself in the legs with some stuff he was preparing for some stupid New Year party joke. New Year party indeed! He'll be lucky if he can walk by the week-end. Put him on his back for a week, that will! I suppose you were in the joke? It's saltpetre that he's shot himself with, of course, though the fool won't admit it!"

It was saltpetre that had been used in the cartridges of Father's gun the night before.

To my great sorrow, I was *not* allowed to be present at the subsequent interview between Father and Blank, the young cowman at the Farm. But I fancy the latter was pretty sorry for himself and his hauntings before that interview was over.

He admitted freely that he had faked the hauntings of the wood for the past two years, and babbled out some story about revenge on the father of the girl who had come to us for help. This man had employed Blank two years before, and had dismissed him for some minor dishonesty.

When Father explained to him that his "ghost-raising" had brought on a nervous breakdown in his former employer, and might have ended in his death, in which case Blank might have had to appear in court on a capital charge, the man broke down and blubbered. He swore never to do anything of the sort again ; agreed to go round that very morning and apologize humbly to the girl and her father ; and gave up the impedimenta of his ghostly impersonations.

We still have these in our Maskelyne museum today. They consist of a sheet with holes cut in it for arms and eyes, some luminous paint of the common phosphorus variety, and a long rope. The latter our "ghost" used to tie to a convenient tree branch, and then, by swinging on the end of it, effect a leap of fifteen feet or so through the air, well above the ground, towards his victim.

I think he suffered pretty severely during the night after he got the saltpetre in his legs. He did not know what the stuff was, of course, and firmly believed he was dying. Anyway, he repented fairly thoroughly of his sins in terrifying a superstitious old man and his helpless daughter ; and he gave no more trouble in the village after that night.

I have had a good many subsequent adventures with

ghosts of one sort and another, as I shall presently tell, but never again have I experienced the horrible thrill that crept over me as I saw the Biddenden "ghost" swing through the woodland glade that night.

I have learned since that there are no such things as ghosts ; and if anyone has any apparitions which require laying, a note, care of my publishers, will bring me along at the earliest possible moment to perform the interesting little ceremony.

If the Pale Lady is getting busy round the ancestral corridors with her head tucked underneath her arm, or Sir Hugh goes clanking his chains up the stairs of the moated grange, or the Cavalier tosses his stingo down while sitting in your best dining-chair, or the miser recounts his shadowy gold at your table—drop me a line. I think I shall be able to prove to you that ghosts—in the real sense— simply don't exist, and to rid you of their worry for ever.

Several times in my career I have met impostors who were cruel and wicked enough to try to reproduce ghostly phenomena for the purpose of terrifying others. But I have never met the real thing in apparitions, and never shall.

To the unfortunates who have been frightened by such things I say in all sincerity—write to me ! You are being victimized either by your nerves or by some criminally minded person who hopes to benefit by frightening you.

I have laid ghosts of both sorts on occasion. So don't let yourself be worried and made nervous and ill any more —just write and tell me all about it. I will treat the letter in confidence, and help you if I can. And I am perfectly sure I can.

CHAPTER X

THE war, which caused such notable bodies as the Admiralty and Military Intelligence to call in the assistance of Maskelynes' Mysteries, also brought great trouble to St. George's Hall.

Mr. Devant, who had gone from triumph to triumph in the years immediately preceding 1914, began to show signs of a nervous breakdown before the war had been in progress many months. On the advice of his doctors, he eventually parted with his interests in Maskelynes' Theatre, the control of which reverted once more to my grandfather, who, despite his advanced years, was as indomitable as ever.

The retirement of Mr. Devant at the very climax of his wonderful career was the more regrettable because he had done so much during his lifetime to bring honour on the whole profession of magic. Only a few short months before he left us a great gathering of magicians from America, France, Germany, England and elsewhere had presented him with an illuminated address of appreciation of his services to wizardry, and accompanied it with a fine service of silver-plate.

The presentation was made at St. George's Hall, in the presence of over four hundred of the leading conjurers of the world.

J. N. carried on at St. George's Hall, with my father to assist him, and for a time the programme ran as sparklingly as ever. But the work of managing the theatre and its multitudinous inside and outside interests was too much for my grandfather, who had already long passed the three-score-and-ten years allotted by the psalmist.

Just as active as ever both in the workshops where our apparatus was built and on the stage itself, J. N. still worked about eighteen hours and slept only six out of the twenty-four. In addition, he took an intense interest in the progress of the war, and continually busied himself with inventions, some of which might have made his name famous on the battlefield had he lived to perfect them.

But in 1917, without showing any preliminary signs of coming collapse, he called my father to him one day.

"Nevil," he said quietly, "I think my work is nearly finished. I have enjoyed my life—the work of it, the triumphs of it, even the troubles and the defeats. There is only one thing now which puzzles me.

"You know I have always opposed spiritualism, and have exposed a good many fraudulent mediums. But famous and learned men—men like Conan Doyle and Lodge—have apparently been convinced that there is something genuine in the belief. It is, I suppose, possible that they may be right. I intend to try to find out.

"Listen, now. When I die, I shall make a very great effort, if it is permitted for dead people to do so, to establish contact with you, and assure you of the reality of spiritualistic teachings.

"I want you, after I have died, to sleep for a few nights in my bed, surrounded by my most intimate personal effects. You can have a trumpet there, or anything else that spiritualists commonly use.

"*If it is possible at all for converse to take place between the dead and the living, I will establish such contact with you.* Listen for it ; wait for it ; try your hardest to pick up any messages

I may be able to send. We will prove or disprove this matter once and for all."

Two days later, J. N. Maskelyne, Father of Modern Magic, passed peacefully on to whatever existence awaits us beyond the greatest Curtain of all.

My father did exactly as he had been commanded. Every night for a week he slept in J. N.'s bed, surrounded himself by personal objects dear to my grandfather, and by the various impedimenta of the earnest spiritualist. During the nights he lay awake listening for the promised message to tremble into his consciousness.

Towards the end of the time, after eating very little and concentrating his whole mind on the task of receiving any impression broadcast from "the other side", he developed a keen, nervous state which, I think, could not have missed even the faintest "vibrations" directed towards him from beyond the veil of death.

But nothing happened. There were no messages. There were no inexplicable phenomena.

In fact, despite his resolute wish, and the perfect readiness of his son to receive a message, J. N. was unable to communicate with the person then most intimate with him in this world—my grandmother, I should explain, had died shortly before her husband.

The knowledge of this experiment has done more to shake my own belief in spiritualism than anything else I have ever experienced or known. Since then I have carried on the challenge of my grandfather and father that I will reproduce exactly any spiritualistic phenomena that any medium can show to an unprejudiced audience.

I have sought for many years to be admitted to a séance. Always I have been refused this request. Yet I, too, am sincerely ready to be convinced.

Once I wrote to a very famous spiritualist pointing this

out. He replied that I should "spoil the atmosphere of a séance".

As I could not be present myself, I sent to this celebrated gentleman the two slates my grandfather had submitted to "Doctor" Slade. These slates were bound and sealed together in such a way that no human agency could have written on the inner faces of them without leaving signs of having first parted the slates. But surely spirits could do this, since the fourth dimension is admittedly their playground.

The slates were returned to me as blank as they went.

I am, as I say, still willing to be convinced by spiritualism —when I am admitted to a séance, and persuaded by what I see there. Should this happen, I will publicly recant anything I have said against spiritualistic phenomena.

But, in view of my grandfather's attempts to "get through" to my father, and their utter failure, I shall require to convince me something more than table-turning, or voices shouting : "Put down that trumpet !" or vague phantasms such as I can better on any stage.

I have said that my innumerable open challenges to spiritualists have met with no response. I must qualify that statement.

A year or two ago a man wrote to me saying that my grandfather's spirit had communicated with him, and given him a message for me. I saw this man at my London home.

He stated that J. N. had struggled very hard to get through to him at a number of recent séances. He described J. N.'s appearance, and mentioned a number of personal tricks and characteristics that I thought were not known outside the family, save by intimate acquaintances.

Then he said that J. N. had explained to him the workings of a conjuring trick that he used to produce on the stage, and whose secret died with him. The explanation of this trick, I was told, was offered as proof positive that the communication was a genuine one, and not a faked effort on the part of my informer.

I listened to the story until it had ended. Then I explained that the trick in question was one invented by my father, not by J. N., and that the secret had died with the former, not the latter, but that it had been solved a year before our conversation by another famous magician.

After that, I showed my visitor the way to do the vanishing trick down my stairs into the street. He was a most apt pupil, and he vanished for good.

When great men die—and I claim that J. N. was a great man in his own sphere—there is almost always a spiritualistic attempt to produce "messages" from the departed spirits.

I challenge the authenticity of these "messages"!

It is significant that they are apparently seldom or never received direct by any relative or dear one who might reasonably be expected to remain in the consciousness of the departed spirit. No; the messages come to professional mediums, whose names gain notoriety thereby.

There is another side to the question. Often, when mediums claim to have heard from widow's dead sons or girls' dead mothers or lovers, money changes hands before the revelations are finished.

I do not make this accusation out of spite. You have only to look through the police-court records of our country for the past few years to find innumerable examples of what I mean.

Do the spirits of our beloved dead really sell their post-mortem messages? I cannot believe it!

At least, my grandfather never did that!

His death was a very great blow to our family, and to the magic performances with which our name was by this time inextricably connected. St. George's Hall was draped

I

in black; magicians sent condolences and regrets from almost every country in the world.

For indeed a Master Wizard had left us.

The character of J. N. Maskelyne is already written in more enduring characters than I can hope to form. This man was a Napoleon of Illusion, a Cæsar of the stage. Sheerly by the force of his own irresistible personality, he created an entirely new form of public entertainment.

My father stepped pluckily into the gap that J. N.'s death had created. Despite war-time difficulties, he carried on at St. George's Hall, giving magic programmes of no less variety and sparkle than of old. New tricks were constantly being invented; new magicians were employed; the literature and invention of the world were searched for illusions old and new.

But from the very day when my grandfather's personality ceased to pervade Maskelynes' Theatre, the magic of the old name began almost imperceptibly to fade. Something was missing.

Where is the sequel that is as powerful as the masterpiece that begat it? What great man's son was as great as he?

Nor was it only in the theatre that J. N. was missed. For many years he had been supervising experiments carried out by my father in connection with wireless telegraphy. It is correct to say that long before even the world of science had brought such a thing to any sort of practical pitch my grandfather and father had conceived the idea of radio stations which should broadcast popular programmes to the general public, and were working on apparatus that it was hoped would bring this dream into reality.

J. N., with his lightning grasp of any subject that might subsequently be used to entertain his patrons, financed a long series of experiments whose object was to perfect a cheap receiving set of much the same style as is common in almost every household today.

So far did these efforts proceed that a radio company was eventually formed by my father, with the title of the Western Telegraph Company ; and a practical little receiving set was created, which could have been marketed quite cheaply in large quantities.

But unfortunately the time was not yet ripe for such an innovation. It was not of any great use selling receiving sets if there was no Broadcasting Company to send out programmes. At one time the project was actually considered of converting St. George's Hall into such a Broadcasting Station. But the plan was too vast, and needed too much capital, for J. N., at his advanced age, to undertake it.

One finds an amazing example of the perversity of Fate in the fact that, ten or fifteen years later, St. George's Hall was actually bought up by the then all-powerful B.B.C., as a concert-hall from which to broadcast variety programmes and similar material. Had the Western Telegraph Company not been born before its time, I might now be in the position occupied by Sir John Reith, though I feel sure I could not fill it with his Cromwellian effectiveness.

While all these stirring events were happening in London, I was still at school. Like most other boys, I drifted through the conventional school career without any but the vaguest ideas about my future. I had no notion what career I should follow when I left school, and was not trained for anything in particular.

Curiously enough, I had then and have always had a great longing to return to farming. I say "return" to farming ; it will be remembered from my earlier chapters that John Maskelyne, owner of the little Wiltshire farm under the wood, and first of all our family to dabble in high magic, was the son of a long line of yeomen farmers, and that my grandfather, J. N., came of the same farming strain. When I retire from the stage, I am going to buy back the old farm again—for it still stands—and settle down there, even if the Little Gentleman in Black, familiar of sixteenth-century John, should still haunt the place.

When I left school at last, my father called me to him and asked me what I proposed doing for a living. I said hesitantly that I supposed I would have to be a wizard like himself.

"My dear boy," he said solemnly, "I am afraid you will never be a wizard like me. Don't you remember our last appearance on the stage, with Mr. Devant in the Royal Performance at the Palace Theatre? You very nearly spoiled his trick; and if you could spoil a Royal Command Performance, you could spoil anything. Now forget all about the family being magicians, and tell me what you would really *like* to be."

"A farmer!" I responded promptly.

Well, it staggered him a bit, I fancy, but he was not going to admit it. Indeed, he gave me a chance at the thing above all others which I would have chosen as a profession.

I was sent down to a farm near Cheltenham, which belonged to an old friend of the family. Alas! I proved to be just like lots of other youngsters who have found that a job in dreams is quite different from the same job in reality.

To tell you the truth, I had fancied myself swaggering about the ploughland, wearing he-man's corduroys, directing the labours of cattlemen and carters, perhaps giving a hand myself on glorious sunny mornings in the fresh fields, drinking warm creamy milk offered by the freckled comely hands of milkmaids, quaffing nutty ale in the long evenings round great log-fires, judging the ploughing contests, leading in the harvest-home, and cutting a gallant figure at the barn-dance that followed.

In time, I thought, I would take unto myself some jolly, buxom farmer's daughter, who should look after my sturdy little family at home while I rode true and hard to hounds, and grumbled to my neighbours, as we guided our tired beasts back after the kill, about the price of sheep-dip and the state of the corn.

In reality it was all so different! In reality ploughing gives you forty-three different kinds of aches in the back, cows are milked by machinery that goes wrong and creates blue murder if you take your eye off it for half a second, days are spent not hunting but mucking out innumerable cow-byres, and evenings not drinking but in a state of exhausted stupor. In reality, the barn-dances exist only by squalling radio, the farmers' daughters all try to marry out of their class and get away to the towns, and ploughmen and carters evince an unconquerable aversion to any overseeing by novices by the simple method of giving noisy and sanguinary notice on the spot.

All these things I discovered for myself before I had been farming in Wiltshire for a week. Picture me, then, a raw town youth in his most awkward 'teens, far too slenderly built and tenderly nurtured to compete against the local huskies, trying to do incredible things with bulls and milk-carts and agricultural machinery, and suffering from the heavy wit of my companions in arms, from farmer himself right down to the village half-wit who looked after the pigs. The latter, in fact, was the worst of all, because whenever I thought out a really good reply to his sallies, he just went all gibbery, and the point was entirely lost.

It is not necessary here to recount in detail all my adventures "down on the farm". Suffice it to say that I began by mistaking a bull for a cow, and ended by upsetting a milk-float.

In the first adventure, I started boldly crossing a field in which a quiet-looking red animal was browsing. I had to go with a message to my employer, who was working in the Four-Acre Field on the far side of the pasture. Curiously enough, I could see, walking cautiously round the edge of this same pasture, the half-wit to whom I have already referred.

This boy looked after the pigs on the farm, but he was mortally afraid of cows, and had been all his life. I determined to show him, that morning, how groundless his fears were, so I waved nonchalantly to him, and called a greeting, as I walked across the meadow. He shouted something back to me, but as he could not articulate words properly, I was unable to make head or tail of his yells.

At the sound of my voice, the red animal, now about thirty yards from me, raised its head. I reflected that it wore its curls rather close for a cow, but then I was only a townsman unacquainted with country fashions. Then I saw it stare down at its forefeet, and begin a funny little prance with them. I thought it was perhaps trying to scratch up a beetle. Then it bellowed, and started at a swift ambling run towards me.

Then I realized that it was a bull.

And that was how I learned to do the vanishing trick. Not, perhaps, the conventional vanishing trick as performed upon the stage, but a most effective and valuable substitute. I streaked across the field and vanished through the hedge. My assistant (the bull)—well, he assisted me !

When I picked myself up, I found the pig-boy standing beside me. At first I thought he was in a fit—he did occasionally suffer from fits. But on this occasion it was nothing of the sort. He was just laughing.

After I had been about a month on the farm—a month of trial, terror and tribulation—I may be said to have handed in my notice. Actually, it was posted from a town five miles away. . . .

I had been put on to the task of taking milk round to a chain of distant cottages which bought direct from the farm. For this purpose I was given charge of a light milk-float, between the shafts of which pranced a skittish pony. I strove with that pony as Jacob strove with the angel, but it was more skittish after than before.

One misty red autumn afternoon I was driving that skittish pony down a deep lane, conveying the afternoon milking to our customers, when my Pegasus met a bit of paper that was blowing gently along the lane towards us. He then tried to imitate his classic forebear by flying, but the milk-float acted as a sort of anchor.

Personally, I was sorry. I would have preferred him to fly untrammelled. As it was, the float jolted and bounced from one side of the lane to the other. I lay back on the reins and prayed to all my gods that the leather would not part and let me down on the road on the back of my head, and the milk-bottles gave a spirited representation of a cargo of Mills bombs putting a sector of roadway under a devastating barrage.

The runaway stopped eventually outside a village pub facing the local station. I cast no aspersions whatever. By that time, though the land was flowing with milk (I am sorry I cannot say "and honey"), the trap itself was empty. Empty even of me, for, with my present bruises and past record, I did not feel equal to the strain of returning to my master and explaining matters to him. The pony knew its way home unaided (it was that sort of pony!), and, after all, where was the use of my going on working on a farm where all the animals were so very much against me?

I stepped smartly into the station, bought a ticket, and waited for the day's train, which fortunately was its usual half-hour late. When it arrived, I got into a carriage and was whirled away at a good ten or fifteen miles an hour to the nearest Big City. There I had friends, including a young fellow of about my own age with whom I had previously discussed some such dramatic ending of my farming career.

"If you ever do it, Jasper," he had said to me a week or so previously, "come straight to me. We can put you up for a night or two, and I'm pretty sure I can get you a job with me, on the road."

Thus it was that I ceased to be a farmer, and became— for positively a few appearances only—the attendant imp on an extra-large steam-roller cruising Jove-like at two miles per hour along the leafy Wiltshire lanes.

CHAPTER XI

My period of service on a steam-roller was even shorter than that spent on the farm. If I was not born an actor, at least I seem to have had no natural aptitude for anything else.

I enjoyed it very much while it lasted. Sitting up on high, in Olympian oblivion of such passing traffic as one might see in those immediate post-war days, I helped to roll out the Wiltshire roads, made abstruse studies of the properties of macadam, gravel, chipped flints, sand and other useful materials, and learned how road-surfaces "flow" downhill under heavy traffic.

I might have gone on and prospered and today been writing a treatise on English roads, but a kindly or unkindly Fate intervened. One foggy evening, returning home on my mighty steed, I wandered clean off the road into a patch of unfenced marshland. The first I knew of the business was that the steam-roller, despite snorts and pantings and a great revolving of wheels, refused to move forward, and began settling steadily and overpoweringly into a deep muddy wallow of its own creation.

A week later, it having been demonstrated to me meanwhile that I should never make a first-class rollerman, I found myself in Essex, running a farm with a friend of mine. This time I had nothing to do with the dairy department, my genius being devoted to turnips, mangolds and other root crops of peculiarly unpleasant habits.

To lighten my labours, I carried out extensive experiments in electricity, in which I was becoming extremely interested. Had I been apprenticed to an electrician, I am fairly certain I should never have made my début on the stage, but by the perversity of things this very hobby brought me my first theatrical success.

Just before my first Christmas in Essex, an amateur dramatic society decided to give a performance of *Babes in the Wood*, at Roydon. They viewed the village hall where the show was to be given, and were disgusted to discover that it was not equipped with any proper lighting facilities. Main electricity was available, but the place was not fitted for it ; and, as any stage-person will assure you, the finest possible performance can be ruined by improper lighting.

Boldly enough, considering my very slight experience, I offered to bridge the gap. I volunteered to wire the hall for electricity, and get everything ship-shape in time for the final rehearsals. The amazing thing is that I was entrusted with the job.

The hall resounded with the tap of hammers and the grating song of the saw ; wire cables whirled within like the feelers of a mad cuttle-fish ; but gradually chaos was reduced to order. A full week before Christmas I was able to sweep up the litter and sawdust, and then proudly conduct the panto-producer right through· the brilliantly lighted hall to the stage, which was now equipped with footlights, dimmers, spotlights and everything necessary to a first-class dramatic performance.

Imagine me, on the occasion of the rehearsal that evening, sitting high up in the flies above the heads of the company on the stage, crawling precariously to and fro, checking this and tightening that, making finally certain that the "lighting by Maskelyne" was perfectly in order.

Below me, in mufti, the actors and actresses rehearsed

the pantomime in that (to the layman) entirely unintelligible fashion that precedes dress rehearsals. They put imaginary hats on invisible tables, to suit the action of the piece, stated that they were sitting down or standing up according as the affair needed such gyrations, and in the intervals of saying their lines they discussed all sorts of irrelevant matters until the producer's sharp : "Now, we'll just run right through that again !" recalled them to attention.

It seemed to me that one part—that of "Robin Hood"— was being badly performed. The actor needed constant prompting ; he did not know his gestures and actions any better than his lines ; and when he finally had to kiss the heroine, I was thoroughly disgusted at the lackadaisical way he did it.

"If I couldn't kiss better than that, I'd take lessons !"

I must have uttered the thought aloud, for I nearly fell off my exalted perch at the sound of my own voice.

The rehearsal below stopped as if the players had turned to stone.

"Who said that ?" inquired the wrathful voice of the stage-manager from beneath.

Since there was no help for it, I slid down a rope on to the stage, and admitted my guilt, apologizing at the same time to the actor I had libelled.

"But I think I agree with you, my friend," he smiled. "You see, I've been dragged into taking this part by George here" (he indicated the stage-manager) "because the man who was doing it has gone and got influenza. I'm only too anxious to retire if we can get a substitute. Why don't *you* have a shot at it ?"

"Yes—why not ?" put in the stage-manager.

I can only suppose that my efforts with the lighting had turned their brains with gratitude, for they meant it seriously. In those days, I was never averse to taking a chance, so I asked for a copy of the "sides" of the part, and started in there and then.

By Christmas I was word-perfect, and the part of "Robin Hood" was politely handed over to me.

The great occasion of the opening night came, and whatever else I did wrong, I flatter myself that I managed to kiss the heroine very realistically indeed.

Next morning I was surprised to see that the local papers, in writing up the show, had all given me a personal mention, not only for my lighting effects but for the way I had played my part. Some of the reports were quite eulogistic! Indeed, I have kept them to this day, so favourable were they.

I was naturally pleased at my success, the more since learning the part in the very short time at my disposal had been a difficult matter. On the second night of the show I put all that was in me into my performance, and really made rather a good job of it.

Afterwards, an astonishing thing happened. I was told that a gentleman wanted to see me, but would not give his name.

"It's my belief he's one of the London theatre managers," whispered our producer, who had brought the message to me. "He's got a top-hat on, anyway!"

And a London theatre manager he proved. For my mysterious visitor was no less a person than Nevil Maskelyne, Managing Director of St. George's Hall, and—my father!

"I saw the Press notices about your performance last night, Jasper," he said. "You didn't know the *Morning Post* had a word about you, did you! So I ran down tonight to see the show, just to get an idea what you were really like."

"And was I all right?" I asked anxiously, knowing him for my most severe critic.

"Pretty good!" he said musingly. "In fact—well, if you like, Jasper, my boy, you can come back and join me at St. George's Hall."

If I liked! Shades of the turnips and mangold-wurzels!

And this was how I came to "go on the stage" as a profession. I have never regretted it.

Let me deviate for a moment. Emphatically I did not like farming when I was a youth and had to do it for a living. Yet the old hankering to be what is loosely termed a "gentleman farmer" survived and grew within me, and it is there yet.

As soon as I could afford to do so, I took a holiday from my stage duties and went back to farming for a change and a rest. It wasn't much of a rest, but during the time I entered a six-counties ploughing contest and won the title of second-best ploughman there. I shall not be content till I have won such a contest, and, later, till I have cut out a niche for myself in West-Country farm life.

To return to the story of Maskelynes.

At St. George's Hall I found the apprenticeship no less fatiguing and lengthy than that which farming had offered me. I returned to London big with ambition, promising myself all sorts of successes which should eclipse my amateur provincial beginning.

"This brilliant young actor", and "a worthy grandson of the founder of Maskelynes", were phrases that I thought already as good as in print. But the path to fame proved a long and arduous one after all.

For two years I was not allowed to set foot on the St. George's Hall stage, save in the capacity of scene-shifter, assistant behind the scenes, and general man-of-all-work.

During the first year, I spent almost all my time in the vast workshops behind the scenes. The carpenter's bench and the lathe temporarily ousted the masks of comedy and tragedy. I was made familiar with the "mechanics" of our magic ; learned just how the levitation and decapitation and other wonderful illusions were performed, worked endlessly at apparatus, some of it as big as a small house and some so minute that it could be hidden behind a wrist-watch.

The machinery of magic is extraordinarily interesting. Tricks which seem quite impossible to perform become elementary once you have mastered the construction of the apparatus used. Every illusion has its own apparatus.

You can apparently cut off a man's head, in full view of the audience, make the head converse with the trunk, raise the body into the air merely at a word of command, pass a steel hoop round the levitated body to show that it is quite unsupported, cause persons to disappear while actually being held by onlookers, make dead hands write and skulls speak, cause a lamp to fly lighted through the air, make a watch disappear from one man's pocket and appear tied round the neck of a rabbit in the lap of another man, permit a member of the audience to fire at you with a marked bullet from a real revolver and catch the bullet between your teeth . . . but why go on ?

I could enumerate all the tricks in the magic calendar, some so astounding as to be disbelieved until actually seen. And in each case the apparatus does the trick, and the more complicated the illusion, the more simple as a rule is the apparatus.

After a year "learning the works", I was permitted to go up into the flies above the St. George's Hall stage, night after night, and watch the tricks actually being performed by master wizards. From above, the machinery of illusions is usually clearly visible.

To all would-be magicians I would recommend a few months in the flies, learning as I did, before anything at all ambitious is attempted on the stage itself.

At this time the world was thrilled by the news of the discoveries in Tut-ankh-amen's tomb at Luxor, in the Valley of the Kings.

For some reason, that fickle jade public fancy indulged for a month or two in a wild flirtation with elementary Egyptology. Every detail of the discovery was avidly read, photographs showing the tomb and the finds filled our papers, and King Tut became "news" in a bigger sense than could ever have happened during his august life.

A very large part of the public interest was aroused through an idle tale that a legend had been found in the tomb roughly equivalent to that left by Shakespeare in his epitaph : "Curst be he that moves my bones !"

Lord Carnarvon's death lent fuel to the fire of superstition, and when it was followed—mainly in the course of nature—by several other deaths among relatives of the investigators, why, then that became "news" too !

Egyptian tombs and tomb-robbers were the topic of the day ; and St. George's Hall, always ready to reflect public opinion, instantly staged a magic playlet, written by my father and entitled *The Scarab*, in which direct reference was made to this fascinating subject.

In the sketch, an archæologist discusses with a dealer the sale of a mummy of King Ra-Thur of Egypt, but proceedings are complicated by the appearance of Joe Billiboy, a burglar, who tries to steal the valuable mummy, and the coming-to-life of the 8000-year-old royalty who is the principal in these affairs.

I was given my first professional stage part as Joe Billiboy, and earned £3 a week for playing it.

It was simple and easy enough, and consisted chiefly in my making a dramatic appearance in the Egyptologist's study, clad in a Bill Sikes cap and muffler. I took very little part in the numerous magic transformations and illusions that provided the real thrills of the playlet; but for me it was a great occasion none the less.

I was now an actor; I was facing the footlights in real earnest; and no subsequent excitement quite compares with this!

For a month or two life now ran smoothly for me. I was absolutely immersed in my stage work; at last I had found the one job in the world for which I was fitted and in which I had a deep and abiding interest. My performances were consistent, though I was not as yet entrusted with anything very important.

Then, one night, I ran up against the sort of mishap which would have made something of a sensation if the public had ever got to know of it; my job was to prevent such knowledge from spreading outside the theatre.

We were presenting a trick with a donkey, but the donkey disappeared before its time. My father was on the stage, and I was behind the scenes waiting to go on, when an agitated magician came running up.

"My donkey's disappeared!" he gasped. "Some fool's left the door open at the back, and the damned beast has vanished. We're due to go on in five minutes. What shall we do?"

I hastily dashed off a note to my father, said a word to the stage-manager, arranging with him to alter the order of the programme, and, assisted by two clowns in full make-up, raced out into Langham Place to try to trace the lost quadruped.

Urgently seeking news of the missing brother, I was presently joined by no fewer than five policemen, and we presently ran him to ground nearly half a mile away, in Berners Street, where he was walking sedately along, apparently wondering whether Oxford Street itself would be too hectic for one so unused to the exigencies of city life.

The donkey, escorted back to the theatre by the five constables, two clowns and myself, arrived in time to be included as the penultimate turn of the evening. He "did his stuff" perfectly, apparently quite unaffected by his taste of urban excitements.

One of the earliest things I learned about magic was that one must be just as careful while rehearsing it as when producing it on the stage. This lesson was brought home rather sharply to me by a curious happening.

Shortly before Christmas, 1924, we decided to introduce into the St. George's Hall programme a topical sketch in which ghosts were raised and laid. The family has always been rather good at producing ghosts, and we practised methods whereby, at a word of command, grey vapour appeared and materialized into a transparent draped figure, candles and lamps were extinguished as if at the touch of a cold phantom hand, and the spectre talked in the conventional hollow voice and uttered dreadful warnings to all and sundry.

I was trying out this trick one morning in the workshops by myself, and had raised a very creditable Pale Lady to whom I was conversing, when a sudden shrill scream interrupted me with such suddenness that I almost fell off the carpenter's bench on which I was sitting. The scream was followed by the sound of retreating feet and the slam of a distant door.

The intruder, whoever he was, had left behind on the floor a perfectly good silk hat.

I went and picked it up, and found inside it the name of an old and valued friend of the family, who lived in the country but occasionally ran up to town for a little holiday. I knew the hotel where he always stayed, so I took a taxi there at once, carrying the hat with me.

"I've never had such a ghastly shock in my life, Jasper,

K

my boy !" my friend exclaimed when I was shown in to him. "I know you fellows do amazing tricks, and I can only suppose the—the thing—I saw you talking to was one of your illusions.

"But the fact is, I had dropped in to see you, and I was thinking of something quite different, and to see that dreadful shape standing there listening to you—well, I was half-way to Oxford Circus before I realized that I had taken to my heels. It's uncanny, my boy—hardly Christian, in fact."

He was still quite white in the face, and I fancy the unexpectedness of meeting a ghost like that in broad daylight was even more of a shock to him than he would confess, though probably had I been able to warn him before he saw it he would have laughed at it just as I did myself.

This same Christmas was notable in the annals of St. George's Hall for the visit there of a party of Lamas who were visiting England from Tibet with the object of checking up their wide book-knowledge of the Western world.

Since these Lamas, in their own way, are about as important as Cardinals in the Church of Rome or Bishops in our own Church, it was naturally a great occasion for us when they indicated that they would like to attend a private performance of English magic at our theatre. Tibet is famous for its wizards, and the Lamas themselves are credited by reliable authorities with being able to "die" and be buried for many months, coming to life again when dug up, and also with being able to raise the dead, to exist without food or drink, and with other apparently magical powers.

Behind the curtain we were on our toes when the eighteen queerly robed figures filed gravely into the stalls of the empty theatre, and we determined to give them a really wonderful feast of wizardry. If my memory serves me rightly, we did our levitation trick (the Lamas are said to be masters of levitation themselves), the illusion in which dismembered limbs and trunk are joined together and become a real man, decapitation, ghost-raising, a trick in which weapons are thrust through a coffin containing a girl and the girl vanishes, and the illusion in which a girl is apparently drawn through a two-inch hole in a big steel plate.

Throughout the performance the Lamas sat silent and impassive. No change of expression lighted their faces. They might have been graven images.

But afterwards, the Chief Lama came round to thank my father for his courtesy in making them his guests for the evening. At the same time he uttered a word of warning.

"These things which you showed us are very great magic," he said slowly. "You and your sons must be very wonderful wizards, and I think you are playing with Powers whose strength you do not know, or you would not raise them thus for the amusement of the impious.

"We cannot understand how it is that a man of knowledge like yourself should be content to give that knowledge unchecked to the world, as you do. Believe me, O Master, if you ever come to Tibet, you will either be shut up in one of the greater monasteries where your gifts can be practised away from the sight of common eyes, or you will be fed slowly into little fires until you die."

And with a wonderful obeisance the old man left us.

Since then I have been on many tours, but I have never been to the Far East. There was something in his voice, and something even worse in his eyes, that one cannot forget.

During the performance of the illusion in which a girl

is apparently drawn through a two-inch hole in a steel plate, the Lamas were invited up on to the stage to watch from close quarters. It was an impressive moment for me when the whole eighteen of them wordlessly trooped up, with a swish and rustle of robes, and arranged themselves in a circle about myself and my assistant, leaving the auditorium vacant.

This illusion is widely known as "Through the Eye of a Needle". A 60-gallon barrel, open at one end, was placed on a small rug on the stage. The Lamas examined the stage, rug and barrel. On the open top of the barrel, which was upright, a riveted steel boiler-plate, one and a half inches thick, was rested. In the centre of this plate was a hole two inches in diameter. The plate was examined by the Lamas. This plate weighed about 90 lbs. and contained 240 rivets.

Then my assistant stood on top of the boiler-plate while the Lamas examined the belt round her waist. This belt had two interlocking rings instead of the usual buckle ; these rings were tied with rope by the Lamas, who sealed the knots with strange heavy seals of their own. On each ring they tied a length of strong sash-cord twenty feet long, and again sealed the knots that held the cord to the rings.

One cord was now passed down through the hole in the steel plate and out of the bung-hole of the barrel below. Another 60-gallon barrel, previously examined, this one having neither top nor bottom, was now placed by the Chief Lama over the head of my assistant, and rested on the steel plate, which itself rested on the lower barrel. The second sash-cord was then drawn through the bung-hole of the upper barrel. A handkerchief was now tied on the rope tight against the lower bung-hole, and another was pinned to my assistant's collar and left hanging loose over the top edge of the upper barrel.

The Lamas now peeped into the top barrel to see that my assistant was still there ; a lid was placed over her ; and a Lama took each blind-cord. He who held the lower cord pulled, and the one holding the upper cord slacked it out.

Instantly the two handkerchiefs began to move—the one on the lower cord coming away from the bung-hole and the other sliding down out of sight into the top barrel.

The girl was being pulled through the two-inch hole in the massive boiler-plate !

When the lower rope could be pulled no more, the Lamas forgot their dignity and *ran* to the apparatus. You must remember that they had been sitting round in a circle meanwhile. They lifted off the lid and looked in the top barrel.

Guttural ejaculations told that it was empty !

They lifted it off, flinging it recklessly along the cord, whose other end could be seen passing down through the boiler-plate into the lower barrel. They strained at the steel plate itself, and set it down on the stage.

There was my assistant in the lower barrel, the cords still passing—one out through the lower bung, the other up through the boiler-plate and the upper bung. Quite obviously, since their queer Eastern seals were still untouched on her girdle, she had been drawn down through that steel plate.

The grave priests were quite overcome. They muttered among themselves and drew uneasily away from me. Finally, the interpreter asked me to repeat the trick.

We did it three times before they were satisfied—I believe they would have liked the performance to go on all day !

Before we left the stage the interpreter gave me a warning similar to that later offered to my father.

"In Tibet," he said ingratiatingly, "we should think you very great Master! If you no enter monastery, we put you in barrel, drive many spikes therein, and roll you down into the great river, for so we treat mighty devils in our land. But perhaps you would enter a monastery, O Master!"

I admitted that perhaps I would.

My assistant in this illusion was a young lady named Evelyn Home-Douglas, who had only very recently joined us. After "passing" her through the steel plate a few times, I felt an impulse quite new to me in my career as a wizard —to follow her through the hole, or wherever else she might go in this old world that had suddenly become so dull without her but so gay when she was near.

This I recognized as *real* magic, so I followed the tradition of the family (and of Mr. Devant), and married within the profession, though only just, for she left the stage when we married, though her sister Cecil helped me in the show for over five years.

Now, in addition to looking after our youngsters, Alistair and Jasmine, she designs all my stage settings that you see up and down the country, and is my ultimate guide and critic in all business matters. Many a time I have had cause to bless the day that provided me with such a fine business adviser, and such a loyal, splendid pal.

CHAPTER XII

Magic in the past—Black Magic still lives—Werewolves and Vampires
—A history of wizardry—Tests for Satanists—Rasputin—Magical
evolution—Cagliostro—Pinetti—De Grisi—Houdini.

IN an earlier chapter of this book I promised to say something about Black Magic, both within my own experience
and outside it. During the two years I spent as an apprentice
to Magic, in the nether regions of St. George's Hall, all
my time not actually spent in the workshops or in the flies
above the stage was employed in reading up the subject of
wizardry, black and white.

This, therefore, being the hiatus between my account
of past Maskelynes and the story of my own stage career,
seems an appropriate place in which both to keep my
earlier promise and to tell you something of the very
ancient art of Black Magic.

But do not think, because it is an old belief, that the
world has outgrown Black Magic. There is no shadow of
doubt that it is still practised today, not only in its original
home in Madagascar or by a few primitive negroes terrified
by Voodoo, but in the heart of fashionable London, and
by rich society leaders and powerful business men.

In the circle in which I move by reason of my profession, magic black or white and all its latest manifestations
is necessarily "shop" talk. And I was told, on what seemed
to be undeniable authority, that the death of a famous
millionaire a year or two ago, unexplained by any of the
usual reasons of financial insecurity or ill-health, was
caused by his own terror at certain devilish manifestations

he had raised after being led into the black and horrible paths of modern Diabolism.

The worship of the Goat of Mendes, Baal, Pan, Kali and others of the Devil's accredited henchmen is still carried on, behind closed doors and to the accompaniment of unspeakable orgies and atrocities, by persons who, in the light of day, are apparently benevolent and respectable.

England is a land of scoffers, yet it is not free of the taint. On the Continent, Diabolism is a recognized menace. A trial for witchcraft took place in France as recently as 1926, at which high officers of the Roman Catholic Church attended; and the accused was found guilty.

Reports of Werewolves and Vampires come to us every year from the older lands, such as Russia and the East, and they seem to be vouched for in every particular.

Personally known to me is a highly placed officer in the police service in British North Borneo who not merely believes in Vampires that suck human blood, but claims to have seen one at work, and to have performed the necessary horrible rites on the native corpse to which this Vampire belonged, so that the soul of the dead man could rest.

My informant is a steady-nerved, practical man of immense Eastern experience. Yet he implicitly believes that he dug up a corpse that had been buried nearly a year, and found it fresh and undecayed, with red lips parted and bright eyes open; and that when he cut off its head and thrust a stake through its chest it screamed like a lost soul, and writhed, and that a great black bat fell dead into the open grave beside it.

I know, too, a French police officer, now retired, who was introduced to me by a distinguished French conjurer. This officer solemnly assured me that, in France, England and elsewhere, tiny children are kidnapped every year, to be offered as human sacrifices, with foul and unspeakable rites, to the Devil, to ensure his alliance towards the people who still worship him in secret.

It is not my purpose here to enlarge on the problem of modern Satanism, but rather to attempt a thumb-nail sketch of magic down the ages, of which it is the diabolic present-day manifestation, just as my own White Magic is the civilized child of the wizardry of Merlin and the Good Fairies.

Belief in magic is as old as humanity itself. Buried with mummies seven or eight thousand years old, modern archæologists discover charms and rituals placed beside the corpse to save the soul from the clutching hands of fiends on its last journey from earth into the Unknown.

I have no doubt that the Piltdown Man wore an amulet, though he may have worn nothing else. Relics of incredible age, in Africa, Australia, America, Asia and Europe all testify to the dreaded powers of wizards, human and inhuman.

In Africa today, and in many other places as well, grown men and women take the most extraordinary precautions to propitiate the spirits, and to avert the Evil Eye. After all, how many of my readers would walk under a ladder, spill salt, cross knives, or fail to experience a slight sense of spiritual discomfort at the smashing of a mirror ?

Charms or mascots are worn by half our population in Great Britain, and by nine-tenths of our cars ! When I was a schoolboy, fully half the juniors who were at school with me willingly gave up halfpence and dainties to a slightly deformed boy of our own age who simply stated that he was a sorcerer, and left it at that !

In primitive times the correct setting for the conjurer was not the theatre but the temple. The Old Testament is full of stories of soothsayers and wise men and wizards.

From Pharaoh's magicians to the Witch of Endor, from Joseph telling the meaning of dreams to St. John writing the Revelation, we have almost unbroken records of magic of one sort or another.

Indeed, we have proof positive of uncanny manifestations not only in the Old Testament but in the New. Christ Himself cast out devils; diabolic possession, according to all modern authorities, was not merely what we call epilepsy or madness, but real control of the soul by certain non-human agencies.

There do not lack modern clergy, both of our own and other Churches, who say that this "possession" is still to be met with today, and that certain rare individuals even now have the power to cure it by the laying on of hands.

Contemporary with Old Testament records, we have indisputable accounts of magic being practised in ancient Egypt, in the Maya civilization, among the Aztecs, in the Bantu civilization of Africa, in Greece, Rome, and among the Hun hordes of northern and eastern Europe, to name only a few places.

The Oracle at Delphi is perhaps the most famous example known to us of a magic temple of olden times. But it seems certain that almost all the false religions of the early world were founded on conjuring tricks, legerdemain and illusion.

Temple doors opened of themselves, statues bled or wept or nodded, bells and sistrums sounded when no hand touched them, mystic voices spoke of the future (in suitably ambiguous terms) out of the thin air, scoffers vanished from human ken, plagues and droughts descended upon their cattle, but all went well with those who pleased the gods by contributing generous offerings to the temple staff.

In the midst of this organized robbery by the conjuring

classes, Christianity came like an exploding bomb. Here was a religion that did not depend on sleight-of-hand and mechanical tricks.

And so what had been a world-wide loosely knit fraternity of fraud and illusion was shattered into fragments. The fragments were very hard to destroy, of course; all over the globe today you can find religions still based on the magician's art, whose priests live on the fat of the land while their devotees starve to feed and keep them.

It is said, I believe with accuracy, that nearly all the great Hindu temples nowadays, where the old conjuring tricks are still worked for the benefit of the black credulous, are farmed out on long leases by rich Babu families to the priests who work them. In fact, the relationship between the Babus and the priests is precisely that of the British coalfield owners to the mining companies—a royalty is received on takings.

Since belief in the supernatural dies hard, Christianity, though it lightened the Western world, left a lot of black shadows in holes and corners, and to these the superstitious crawled with a glad fervour. Love-philtres were sold in A.D. 1, and they are sold today in many parts of rural England. Wizards were consulted by the Romans just as wart-charmers are consulted now.

The king-pins of the sorcery trade, however, have always been those brave individuals who professed to dabble in witchcraft pure and simple. Even the alchemists and the astrologers gave precedence to these.

And yet, if the rewards for the successful wizard were great ones, as they undoubtedly were, the price of failure was a heavy one. Now and again, yokels stirred to savagery by long years of robbery and oppression, would turn on the priests of darkness, risking the revenges of all the powers of Hell.

Then away went the witch or magician to the nearest horse-pond, and after a trial which consisted of a lengthy jabbing with pins and knives to see if an insensitive spot could be found (true mark of the touch of the Devil's fingers !), the offender was flung into the water and kept there by the gentle aid of long poles and pitchforks until such time as the rustics had decided whether drowning was possible or impossible.

This was, of course, rather hard on the accused. It was a common belief that a disciple of Satan could not be drowned. Of course, if the unfortunate *did* drown, the supposition was that he or she had been unjustly accused after all. But that was not a lot of use after the drowning had taken place ; and as long as the swimmer kept on the surface, or merely popped below a few times obviously in order to hold private converse with the Father of Lies— well, so long were the poles and pitchforks busily plied, and the test went merrily on.

I have, among my collection of books on magic, an extraordinarily interesting little volume published early in the seventeenth century by one, Joseph Glanvil, entitled *Plain Evidence Concerning Witches and Apparitions*.

This book consists simply of an account of Dr. Glanvil, who was an educated man, and a great friend of Charles, Duke of Richmond and Lennox, of cases of so-called witch-craft, Devil-raising and superhuman possession, most of which had come within his own or his friends' experience. It is an amazing list.

The book contains some intensely interesting descriptions of "Witches' Sabbaths", in which hags and wizards dance naked about old stone altars, lighted by black candles. The Lord's Prayer is chanted backwards, stolen Communion wafers are defiled, feasting and orgies take place —and then, at the climax of the affair, a little gentleman in black silk appears in the midst of the revellers, who fall on their faces about him.

After this, prayers for power or wealth are uttered, wax images of enemies are melted or pierced with pins, and petitions are put forward. Those of the unholy worshippers who wish to haunt or to have power over other people are permitted to fly thence on broomsticks and wands touched by the Devil, and, passing through solid obstacles and travelling immense distances in the winking of an eye, achieve their desires and return instantly to the bodies still lying in worship before the black-clothed Adversary.

I should add that in all the cases mentioned in Glanvil's book the witches and wizards were subsequently tried by educated magistrates and judges of the times, and found guilty of witchcraft, and that most of them perished either by the water-test I have described above or by ordeals still more horrible.

Of these experimentalists in Black Magic, the modern-day Satanists are the spiritual descendants. Diabolism is said to be practised now in an endeavour to attain money and power ; and, so long as the adepts keep themselves to themselves, and do not let the police hear of their soul practices, they are in considerably less danger than were their predecessors of less civilized eras.

Yet resentment to the dark habits of suspected Devil-worshippers dies hard. I remember my grandfather telling me of a case which came within his own notice, and which he mentions in one of his books, wherein a Frenchman living in the Essex village of Sible Hedingham was literally swum to death, after having been kicked and beaten for an hour by men and women, because he was believed to be in league with Satan.

Occasional lynchings of this nature occur even now in

rural England, though they are naturally not reported as such in the Press, since the killers take care that the death of the so-called sorcerer shall seem accidental, or else the work of some untraceable murderer.

In Russia, at least, we have a modern instance of an accredited Satanist, Rasputin, being slaughtered because he was believed to be in league with the Devil. Anyone who has read the amazing book *Rasputin*, by William le Queux, can find chapter and verse for the accusation, and a most vivid description of the superhuman amount of killing that the rascally old monk required, though whether this proved his diabolism or not the author naturally does not say.

While the followers of Black Magic were carrying on their dangerous experiments in this way, the alchemists, astrologers and others were developing the study of magic along more decent lines. Broadly speaking, their researches may be subdivided into two main heads, the effort to discover a method of transmuting base metals into gold and age into eternal youth, and a serious study of prophecy by the aid of the stars.

Astrology developed into astronomy, in which department my ancestor, Nevil Maskelyne, became famous in the time of George III. The alchemists, after a time, subdivided again within their own cabal.

Some became doctors of medicine; some became chemists whose studies were the basis of much that we now know about food, metals, materials and matter generally; and a few—and as I claim these were the purest line of descent—turned illusionists, exchanging the dream of the Philosopher's Stone, that was to turn lead into gold, for the reality of the Mystery Theatre which derives gold from public amusement and entertainment.

The spiritual father of all modern illusionists and white

magicians was undoubtedly Cagliostro, the hero of Dumas's book, *The Memoirs of a Physician*. Son of an Italian peasant, this remarkable man rose to immense fame and riches shortly before the French Revolution. It was said of him at the height of his celebrity that he wore a King's ransom in diamonds as ornaments on his magic robe.

At about the same time Comus I gained notoriety throughout France for his "writing hand". This man later came to London, where he created a sensation.

A little later Pinetti came to London with a really clever thought-reading act. He had with him a little figure about two feet high, which he called the Wise Little Turk, and this figure answered questions concerning articles offered to Pinetti by members of the audience.

Robert Houdin and Heller later developed this thought-reading trick to a pitch that borders on the uncanny. In their presentations, the "seer" sat blindfold on the stage while the assistant took an article from the audience.

Suppose the article was a seal. The "seer" would tell, in answer to questions, of what metal and what stone the seal was made, the initials on it, how they were engraved, the approximate weight of the seal, the type of chain on which it was hung, the sex and approximate age of the owner, the colour and cut of his clothes, and all without receiving any apparent suggestion of a "pointer" from the questions asked by the assistant.

The whole secret is that such thought-readers, before they appear on the stage, learn a very lengthy and complicated code. In this code, the letters in such stock questions as "What is that?" or "The maker's name?" stand for prearranged words giving the clues to the answers desired by the assistant.

It takes two or three years of intensive study to learn one of these codes, as may be guessed, since the objects offered for identification by the audience are in no way restricted, and the "seer" must answer swift as lightning or the whole thrill of the trick is lost.

At the height of his fame, Pinetti, founder of thought-reading tricks, gave a performance in Naples. A young French exile, the Comte de Grisi, an amateur conjurer, later repeated several of Pinetti's tricks at a party for the amusement of his friends.

Pinetti heard of this and was furious. He developed a sham friendship with de Grisi, persuaded the latter one evening to take his place on the stage in Naples, and then succeeded, by means of a sleight-of-hand, in introducing a pack of marked cards into the impedimenta with which the amateur was going to perform.

Presently de Grisi went up to the box of the King of Naples, who was present at the show, and asked him to draw a card from the pack, as part of a trick he was performing. The King drew out a card at random, but found that it was pencilled across with an obscene lampoon concerning himself. He immediately left the theatre, causing a great sensation.

De Grisi was ruined and exiled. He then sold his family heirlooms and jewellery, and with the proceeds took lessons under the most famous conjurers of the day. At the end of a year he was ready for his revenge on Pinetti.

He followed his enemy round from town to town, giving much better performances in each place. Pinetti lost his reputation, became a laughing-stock, and died of starvation.

De Grisi, however, was not to find final happiness in magic. He attained a great reputation after giving a performance before an audience of Cardinals in Rome, but shortly afterwards his only son was shot while appearing on the stage, a real bullet being placed among some sham ones used in a trick in which his father appeared to fire at him with a matchlock. It was said that a nephew of Pinetti's was responsible for the substitution that resulted in the tragedy.

The wounded youth died almost at once, and de Grisi, utterly broken up by his part in the affair, never appeared before the public again, and very soon afterwards he also died of a broken heart.

Before he passed away, however, he had handed on the torch direct by training a French lad, Robert Houdin, who was later to become one of the greatest illusionists of all time.

By means of an apparatus whose secret was explained to him by de Grisi, Houdin enabled a French nobleman to catch in the act a servant who had been systematically robbing him for two years. This man had stolen some 20,000 francs, but the money was recovered, and the nobleman loaned it to Houdin, who used it to start in Paris a French forerunner of what Maskelynes' Theatre later became in London.

Houdin used electricity for a number of his tricks, and as it was then almost unknown to the public, he was naturally able to create some astonishing illusions. He reproduced the Fakirs' tricks of making a date-palm grow from a stone under the eyes of the audience ; he produced talking skulls and spirit cashboxes, and some exquisite tricks with animals and birds.

After Houdin came Anderson, the self-styled "Wizard of the North" ; Pepper—now immortal for "Pepper's Ghost", a clever illusion worked with mirrors ; and then J. N. Maskelyne.

Before my own initiation into the mysteries of White Magic, I spent innumerable hours studying the works of these past-masters. My researches took me as far afield as

L

the British Museum (whose Egyptian papyri translations have furnished me with the secrets of tricks practised before the Pharaohs and which I have since successfully revived), the private collections of men famous and obscure who have made a life-study of necromancy and illusion, and to many queerer places still.

To this day I still pursue any out-of-the-way bit of knowledge about present or past wizardry. I shall always do so. For a stage magician, if he is to keep really abreast of his work, and to carry forward his minute personal part of the world study of magic, must do far more than just produce pretty illusions before the footlights.

His work must be a world-wide search for mystery, natural or supernatural; and if he succeeds, even by one iota, in his lifetime, in throwing the light of reason on to the dark spots of human superstition and misguided credulity, then he may fairly hope to be accounted a success by his peers in the magic world.

CHAPTER XIII

An all-in wrestling match with a Co-Optimist—A canary that wouldn't
vanish—Why I use rubber animals—Death of Nevil Maskelyne—
Lightning at his burial—I become Managing Director of St.
George's Hall.

ONE of the first big illusions presented on the stage in
which my future wife helped me was the cause of a little
excitement on the occasion of its first appearance.

In this trick I invited a committee of strangers from the
audience to come up on the stage, so as to see for themselves that there was no obvious spoof in the performance.
Now, it is a fixed idea of those exasperating persons who
believe that they can explain away "how it is done" from
the beginning to the end of the magician's calendar that
these committees are stage-hands in the pay of the illusionist, and that though they see the works of every trick, they
just pretend not to do so, in order to delude the audience.

I have even met people who declare that they have seen
my performances in various theatres, and that the committees I invite on to the stage are always the same men ;
presumably these individuals travel round with me for the
love of the thing, since I certainly do not pay them to
do so !

However, at the performance at St. George's Hall of
which I am speaking, there was certainly one member of
the committee who was not secretly in my pay, and that
was David Burnaby of the Co-Optimists.

When he climbed on to the stage, he was greeted with
a cheer ; for at that time London was very proud of its
Co-Optimists, who had boldly put on a play on the share

system, the company risking their savings and their salaries on the success of their work—with what golden reward for courage the whole world now knows.

I placed my committee here and there about the stage, giving them their own choice of position up to a certain point. The trick I proposed doing was to place Miss Home-Douglas inside a cannon on the stage, fire the cannon at a nest of boxes which hung from the theatre ceiling, high above the heads of the audience; and then, hey presto! the cannon was empty and the lady was found in the middle of the nest of boxes.

Mr. Burnaby suggested that he would like to put his hand on the mouth of the cannon, as I fired it, so that his hand would be struck aside by my "human cannon-ball" as she hurtled through the muzzle on her way into the suspended boxes.

Now, with an ordinary committee member, I might have had no objection to offer to this course, except to warn the daring one that his hand might be badly hurt. But Mr. Burnaby is, as I happened to know, a distinguished amateur illusionist himself. An ordinary member of the public could have stood there and been no wiser—though probably sadder—at the end. But I was afraid that Mr. Burnaby, with his shrewd knowledge of illusion apparatus, might guess rather more of the "works" of the trick than I was prepared to show, since it was one of our best feats at the time.

Mr. Burnaby, however, was as determined to choose his own place on the stage as I was not to allow him to do so! In the end, we had a sort of friendly hand-to-hand struggle (all-in wrestling à la mode!), and Mr. Burnaby, being much bigger and heavier than I am, beat me hands down.

But then he was too much of a sportsman to take

advantage of his victory. The trick proceeded ; I fired the cannon ; when the smoke cleared away there was my assistant some sixty feet above our heads, in the basket-nest, high above the auditorium. And Mr. Burnaby's hand and my reputation were still intact.

Such little difficulties as this are the pepper of a stage magician's life.

I had another pinch of pepper within a couple of days of this incident. I was producing the disappearing bird-cage illusion, first invented by Bautier de Kolta in my grandfather's time.

To perform this trick I came on to the stage carrying an ordinary wire bird-cage containing a canary. It was a rubber canary ; this does not affect the trick, as it is just as easy to perform with a live bird. I will explain my choice later. Anyway, even the rubber bird could hop about and twitter.

Passing down the bird-cage to any member of the audience who wished to examine it thoroughly for himself, I then took it in my hands again, and offered to throw it to anyone who was cricketer enough to catch it. Selecting from the half-dozen replies I received, I swung the cage through the air three times, and, on the third swing, it left my hand and flew towards the patron who had offered to catch it.

But when I asked if he had received it, he replied in the negative. Apparently astounded, I stepped down into the stalls, walked to his seat, and looked about for the cage, though without success. Then I asked him if he thought I had the cage hidden under my coat.

Usually, the answer to this question was a laughing one that a magician might have anything under his coat ! So I took off my coat, passed it round among the audience for examination, and it was finally returned to me with the

guarantee that there was neither bird nor bird-cage concealed within its folds or lining.

Tossing it negligently over my arm, I noticed immediately that it would not lie flat ; in fact, that the outline
of a cage was visible under it, and that the twittering of
the canary could again be heard.

Lifting the jacket in astonishment I revealed the cage,
with bird inside all complete within it.

That, at least, is how the trick goes *when* it goes ! On
this night in particular it went, but went wrong !

I showed the cage to the audience, received it back
again, and stood before the footlights swinging the cage
towards the selected patron who had offered to catch it.
On the third swing the cage left my hand in a manner quite
contrary to what I had intended.

There was no need to ask whether my amateur assistant
had caught it or not ; he could not have been much of a
cricketer after all, and he did *not* catch it. Instead, it crashed
into the back of a seat, narrowly missing an old lady's
bonnet, and fell in a crumpled heap to the floor.

Because of such possibilities, I do not use live birds ;
there is also another reason, as I shall explain presently.

I ran down to the place where the bent and broken cage
was lying, and picked it up. Everyone was tremendously
interested, and unkindly anxious to see a magician caught
out at last !

"Ladies and gentlemen," I announced, "of course you
are all aware that I did not mean to throw the cage as
clumsily as that. As you see, it is bent and twisted out of
shape."

I called a stage-hand down, and gave the remains to
him, telling him to take them behind the scenes, which
he did. Then I turned to the audience again.

"Of course," I said, "I cannot offer you such a ruinous

bird-cage as that for your final inspection. But, being a *real* magician, I don't see what is to prevent me from producing a perfect one in its place, out of the air."

I took off my jacket and passed it round. It was returned to me with the usual guarantee that it had "nothing up its sleeve". I then cast it over my arm—when the bird-cage shape appeared underneath it, and lo and behold! (as Moses, that Master Magician, used to say), there was an undamaged bird-cage and a perfect rubber canary chirping away as if it could not get its notes out fast enough.

The audience was rather pleased with that!

Now as to this affair of rubber animals. I never use live birds or beasts or fishes on the stage unless the conditions are such that it can be clearly proved that they are neither hurt nor frightened by their sudden publicity.

This is not the case in the disappearing bird-cage illusion.

Some time ago a very famous and clever magician was accused of hurting the canaries he used in this trick. He replied that he did not hurt them, and that he could prove his words.

I believe the case eventually went to Court, and that it ended in the House of Lords. There followed the rather curious incident of a conjurer performing an illusion before a breathless assembly of peers and bishops, in England's oldest house of government.

The magician performed the vanishing bird-cage trick perfectly, and the canary he used was afterwards examined and found to be quite uninjured.

But—and it is a big but in my mind—I do not see how anyone could perform this illusion without terrifying the bird used. I am prepared to admit that it is a matter of opinion, but it is my opinion, and I stick to it.

Moreover, although the magician in question was successful in not hurting the canary, I could not guarantee to perform that illusion half a dozen times without hurting the bird I used. And I consider myself as quick and skilful a magician as most of my contemporaries.

It is a significant fact, perfectly easy of proof, that when this trick was first performed, and for many years afterwards—in fact, until rubber canaries came into common use—canaries' legs got broken and rebroken time after time in the presentation of this illusion.

De Kolta, inventor of the trick, himself changed his method so as to use a rubber bird, because, he said, the trick was almost impossible to perform swiftly without breaking the canary's legs.

For years, in fact, the birds' legs *were* broken, and mended with match-sticks for the next performance, when match-sticks and legs would be broken again. In such cases, it was usual for the bird to die after about a score of performances, at which its legs were rebroken almost every time.

I cannot doubt that the particular illusionist who took his case to the Lords had a unique and splendid aptitude for this particular trick, and that he never hurt the birds he used. It does sometimes happen that one man can perform one trick better than anyone else. But I have never met anyone else with this ability, and I do not possess it myself.

It was very soon after I became engaged to Miss Home-Douglas that my father, Nevil Maskelyne, died.

He did not, perhaps, achieve as wide a fame as a magician as that attained by my grandfather. But, then, J. N. was as great a man in his own especial sphere as Lord Northcliffe was in journalism or Marconi in wireless telegraphy.

Nevil Maskelyne was a wonderful electrician, tied by tradition to the bricks and mortar of St. George's Hall. Painstakingly and well he taught himself to be a master illusionist, but his heart never thrilled at the glitter of the footlights or the clatter of appreciative applause.

I believe that he might have made a name as famous as that of Marconi had he had the courage of *his* convictions, and, as J. N. himself did, thrown over everything for the one profession on which his mind was set. Instead, he kept one foot in the theatre and one in the laboratory. What my grandfather, whose magic was his life, would have said had his son cut himself off from St. George's Hall I cannot imagine. Yet such a course might have been the happier one in the end.

Before my father died, he repeated to me, almost word for word, the last instruction of his father to him. He said that he wished to convince me about spiritualism—whether it was a great delusion or a strange reality. He asked me to sleep in his bed for a day or two after his passing, and to be ready to receive the slightest message from him, if he could by any chance get into communication with me.

It was an uncanny sensation, resting there, with him lying dead in the house, and waiting for a message from the departed soul of the man who had been—and still is—so dear to me, and so wonderfully and sympathetically my friend.

No message came through.

It has been stated in a leading spiritualist magazine that my grandfather, J. N. Maskelyne, confessed to a well-known surgeon, just before his death: "It is all true. Spiritualism is all true, but I dare not tell the public."

The same statement has been attributed in print to my father.

I would like to say here that it is a foul lie, and an abominable libel, in both cases. No one outside a lunatic asylum or a séance-room would credit my grandfather with being afraid to tell the public—anything.

He believed in the public. Its wishes were his law, its entertainment his life. He was not one of the modern school of artists who believe that it is clever to keep tongue in cheek while serving the public who are their paymasters. He *earned* his money.

Had he been on his death-bed, and been convinced of spiritualism, he would have risen and proclaimed the truth from the housetops. He was incapable of deceit ; his whole life-story shows it.

My father, while less forceful, was equally uncompromising. I knew him better, I think, than anyone except Mother ; and I know that he would have proclaimed himself a spiritualist, had he ever been convinced, even had the announcement rent St. George's Hall in twain.

It is like the spiritualists, as I have seen them, to put yet another bogus statement into the mouth of a dead man. I know there are sincere people among them, and probably also sincere mediums. I have no axe to grind against them ; I would be convinced myself if I could be admitted to a séance at which anything happened that I could not reproduce by conjuring

But they do their case no good by permitting one of their chief periodicals to take advantage of the legal axiom : "You cannot libel a dead man."

When my father was buried a very strange thing happened. It was a dull, cool day, one of those days when Nature seems to drowse.

As the coffin was lowered into the grave, in the family vault at Wandsworth, there came a single terrific peal of thunder, and a ghastly flash of lightning seemed to split the skies and strike like a heavenly scorpion down among the tombstones at our feet.

There was no thunder or lightning anywhere else in England that day ; nor was the single flash and roll repeated.

All the newspapers of the time commented on it as a freak electrical disturbance.

This happening aroused afresh references to the devil-legend of the Maskelyne family, which I have mentioned elsewhere. And the most astonishing thing of all was that almost every newspaper stated that an exactly similar thing had happened, on a day as unlike thunder weather as it was possible to imagine, when another member of the family was buried.

I was very much upset at my father's death, and at having to give my show that night in the theatre and listen to the applause while his dead body lay under the same roof. Perhaps because I was the only member of the family to assist him at St. George's Hall, or possibly through that intimacy which often exists between the head of a house and its younger child, he and I had always wonderfully understood one another, and had been comrades and friends in the deepest sense.

I slept very restlessly for some weeks after. This spell of insomnia was ended in a strange manner. I had tumbled myself into a sort of doze one night, when I thought that I awoke and went down in my pyjamas from the flat I used in the theatre building to the empty and deserted auditorium of St. George's Hall.

It was pitch dark there, but some sort of performance seemed to be going on, and the stage, though all the lights were down, had a strange luminosity which showed me figures moving about on it. I thought at first that this eerie play was being presented without any audience to view it; but quite suddenly I realized my mistake.

The place was crowded; far more crowded than any human audience could have packed it. It seemed to contain millions and millions of presences—a host made possible only by some fourth-dimension miracle. As I walked down towards the front stalls I was hemmed in and crowded. . . .

Then I saw my grandfather sitting in one of the stalls, and my father, and an empty seat was reserved for me between them. They were both in full evening dress, and both looked well and happy; indeed, they were laughing at some joke between themselves.

I sat between them and watched the performance on the stage. It was some sort of a magic play, but it seemed more real than make-believe. Witches were dancing an obscene measure round a great steaming cauldron, their elf-locks flying, their red eyes gleaming like malevolent rubies.

In the steam that rose from the boiling pot I saw strange faces appear—monsters of nightmare shape, headless babies, great bats, and once the head and shoulders of a girl of absolutely unearthly, evil beauty.

The face of this girl awoke me, and I found that I was still in my bed, sweating with fear and excitement. The ruling passion is strong, and beside my bed lay a big diary, always kept there to record ideas that come to me when I am sleepless. I made a few notes of my vision, and then turned over and went to sleep.

Next night I dreamed exactly the same thing; but the dream lasted longer. While I was watching the figures appear in the smoke, my grandfather leaned over to me.

"I'll just tell you how that's done," he whispered.

And then he and my father between them explained to me how to produce an identical illusion.

I woke up again as the last words were being spoken, and there was my note-book ready at my side. In it I entered the details of the illusion; and the very next morning—indeed, I was almost too impatient to wait for daylight—I set to work constructing the apparatus necessary.

When it was ready, I tried it out; and it produced by

far the most life-like effects of this sort that I have ever seen—or should I say witch-like ?

It has ever since been my ambition to produce these effects for the Witches' Scene in *Macbeth*. I was asked to do so on one occasion by a leading producer, but he and I did not see eye to eye about the question of my secret methods. That is to say, I wanted to keep them a secret, while the producer felt that, *as* producer, he ought to "see the works".

So I withdrew ; but I still hope to gratify my ambition one day, and I believe the effect will create something of a sensation when it first appears on the stage.

After my father's death in 1926, I was left with all the real responsibility of St. George's Hall on my shoulders. I was the only one of my generation who had been appearing there regularly, and I had a pretty good idea both of what our public wanted and how to give it to them.

But I was only twenty-four years of age—probably the youngest theatre-manager in London. I had not had enough experience to make me sure of myself in my new role ; and though I later became Managing Director, it was with very considerable qualms.

Presenting magic is one thing ; controlling the destinies of a place with such a tradition as that of St. George's Hall is another.

I combed the world for talent ; I sought out artistes and illusions in the most unlikely places. I worked about twenty hours a day, in the workshops making apparatus, on the stage rehearsing, or actually giving or superintending performances.

I think I did pretty well. We kept receipts up to about normal levels, and kept expenses down to a reasonable figure. We carried on. I think that J. N. himself, in my position, could have tried no harder, though perhaps he might have done more. But then—though I repeat myself— J. N. was a genius.

CHAPTER XIV

Western magic before an Indian Maharajah—"The Dizzy Limit"—
Indian Rope Trick theories—Sword-walking—Two sensations
at St. George's Hall—Tricking the C.I.D.—Secrets of my magic.

In the early months of 1926 I was invited to give a performance of magic before one of the most critical judges who has ever seen me perform. This was no less a person than the Maharajah of Jodhpur.

Ruler of an area of India that is almost as big as England, and descendant of a ruling family that traces its direct ancestry in an unbroken line for nearly a thousand years into the past, the Maharajah's Court is one of the most famous homes of magic in all the East. From a child, he had seen native jugglers and fakirs perform their miracles for his amusement; and now he wanted to watch a representative of Western magic produce something in competition.

A giant marquee was erected for my special benefit on the lawn of the Maharajah's Wimbledon home, and a fine stage was built inside it, complete down to the last detail of lighting and curtaining.

Near the stage was another tent, with a very heavy black veil down one side of it. Just before my show was due to begin, the Maharanee of Jodhpur and her sister were carried, in heavily curtained palanquins, into this small tent, and thereafter they watched my illusions through tiny eye-holes in the black curtain.

It was an eerie feeling, I can assure you, making Western magic under the ever-present spell of watching Eastern eyes.

And I had another incentive, if one was needed, to be "on my toes" that night. This was the first occasion for over fifty years that a member of my family had given a magic show outside St. George's Hall. What an astounding departure from the old tradition that first step was to herald!

The Maharajah, his doctor, and a number of disguished guests sat in the stalls when, at last, the performance was all ready to begin.

I produced the very best illusions I could stage, of course, and two of them interested the Indian potentate particularly.

In the first of them, my assistant, a girl, came on the stage clad in a check wrapper. She climbed into a strong hammock that was swung about eight feet away from the sides and back-cloth of the stage, and about five feet up from the boards. I had formerly held up the hammock so that the audience could see that it was transparent, and that there was no trickery about it.

The girl sat up in the hammock, adjusted her hair, and called to the audience, to show that she was real, and that she was actually in the hammock—in fact, that her presence there was no mere mirror illusion.

Then I fired a revolver at her, the hammock collapsed, the check wrapper floated down to the floor—and the girl vanished, though her scream was heard simultaneously with the report of my pistol.

This trick is called "The Dizzy Limit", and is a speciality of my own. It can be very effective indeed when well performed.

The other trick that took the laurels that evening needed a stone sarcophagus for its performance. This ancient coffin was wheeled on to the stage and examined by a committee from the audience. It was then lifted on to trestles to clear it of the stage and allow free space beneath it, to exclude the chance of a trap-door there.

The sarcophagus had holes in the sides, and was just

large enough to contain my assistant, who climbed into it and lay down. The lid was fitted on, and the whole roped and sealed. My assistant then called to us from inside the coffin ; and indeed she could clearly be seen in there, through the holes, during the whole of the illusion.

Then I handed down to the Maharajah a bundle of spears, swords and long knives, of native Indian workmanship. These he tested in every way possible, to see whether the blades telescoped into the handles, or whether they were faked in any other way. He was, of course, an expert on Indian weapons, and he passed these as being absolutely genuine, sharp and dangerous.

I then took back the knives, swords and spears, and thrust them through the coffin, in at one side and out at the other ; and as each passed through, my assistant within gave a realistic shriek, the cries getting fainter as more and more weapons passed apparently through her body ; for there was obviously no room for her to avoid them in the narrow confines of the coffin.

When the sarcophagus was a veritable hedgehog of bristling weapons, these were withdrawn and the committee from the audience broke the seals and cut the ropes about the coffin. I then raised the lid, and my assistant rose from within, as fresh and undamaged as when she had entered.

I heard a gasp from behind the black curtain at that, and was reminded of the Maharanee who sat there.

"I'll bet you fifty pounds you wouldn't get into that coffin and let him do it to you," the Indian ruler challenged his native doctor, who was sitting next him.

"My price is five millions, sir," was the instant reply.

There was some laughter, but the challenge was not eventually accepted, though the doctor later assisted me very ably in some disappearing-card tricks I wanted to

THE STORY OF MASKELYNES

perform. He would have been quite safe in earning his fifty pounds by lying in the coffin, too, had he only known it!

"You made the girl disappear miraculously—in fact, more marvellously than I have seen even a fakir make anything vanish before," said the Maharajah to me after the performance, when we were chatting on magic. "Can you do the Indian Rope Trick for me?"

But here I had to admit that I was beaten. Neither I nor—as I firmly believe—anyone else in the world can do this trick to conform with the old legend, which I have described fully in Chapter VIII of this book.

I asked my questioner whether he himself had ever seen this trick performed in India or elsewhere.

"No," was the answer. "I have never seen it, though I have searched my dominions for a man who can produce it for me. I am certain it has never been done in the original form of the Indian legend."

Well, there you are! I think that is proof enough that the thing is an impossibility. Yet, on the stage, I believe that we shall one day see the Rope Trick illusion perfectly presented, and I expect to be the man who presents it. You will readily appreciate that doing it on the stage, where apparatus and black velvet together can work many seeming miracles, is quite a different matter from effecting the same illusion in the open air, away from draperies and unassisted by mechanics.

I have my plans perfected now to give a big Indian Rope Trick show, as soon as I can find a suitable theatre and an opportunity to rehearse the illusion thoroughly. I shall never give this trick in the provinces, for an obvious reason. There stage-hands and others who necessarily see something of the works of a big new illusion are always subject to bribery and persuasion from rival magicians who wish to learn the secret of a new trick.

I have lost some exclusive magic that way already, and I do not propose to risk what will, I believe, eventually be one of the biggest "scoops" of my career.

After the performance before the Maharajah of Jodhpur, I repeated in the Press my challenge that I would pay a huge fee, and a very large weekly salary, to anyone who would produce the Indian Rope Trick for me in the open, according to the terms of the legend.

This challenge brought me a curious response. One evening as I was returning about midnight to my home, after a visit to some friends, I found a wizened little figure crouched in a blanket on my doorstep. So small was it that I thought it was a child; but it proved to be a little old Indian.

I took him indoors, and he told me he had seen my challenge, and, though he could not perform the trick I wanted, he had other Eastern illusions in his repertoire that might interest me. He said, incidentally, that he had actually seen the Rope Trick performed in a temple devoted to the worship of Kali, in Eastern Bengal. His explanation was that the fakir who produced it was a master of hypnotism, and that he hypnotized the whole of the congregation present, who had previously been got into a sympathetic state by the swinging censers that spread heavy opium fumes through the temple, and also clouded the atmosphere to a foggy density.

More interesting still, he told me that he had seen a photograph obtained by a Bengali merchant, actually taken during a performance of the Rope Trick. The photograph showed the fakir sitting on the ground in the midst of a circle of onlookers. Of rope or boy there was no sign; yet the merchant swore that he had taken the picture at the moment that the boy was climbing the rope. The idea was that the fakir had simply willed the audience to see things that did not exist—to imagine the trick, in fact. Yet I fail to see how one man could hypnotize a multitude, unless possibly they were prepared, with drugs and religious exaltation, as in the affair described at Kali's temple.

My Indian friend wished to obtain an engagement from me to appear under our banner at St. George's Hall. He had a good repertoire of tricks, but we were at that time fully staffed, and as he had nothing novel to offer, the best I could do for him was to get him a job in a provincial theatre, where I believe he was a great success.

One of his best tricks was "sword-walking". This, and sword-swallowing, since they are not illusions, but are actually performed in all reality, have always struck me as being more marvellous than most of the things that mere conjuring can show.

The sword-walker has a ladder of swords built into a rigid framework, usually about ten feet high, and with a board platform at the top. The swords form the steps of the ladder, and they are placed edge-up. A flag or some similar object is placed on the platform, and the sword-walker goes barefoot up the ladder of weapons, resting his full weight on his naked soles when these are supported only by sword-edges ; yet he is not injured.

A committee from the audience is allowed to examine the ladder beforehand and test the edges of the swords with paper or with the hand ; in fact, such committees not infrequently cut their hands by pressing too hard on the edges of the weapons.

The secret is really very simple. The performer first bathes his feet in a very strong alum solution, to which zinc sulphate is added. The feet are gently dabbed dry, and then plunged into ice-cold water, and dabbed dry once more. They will then resist almost any cutting edge.

In 1926 I spent a good deal of time exploring the

possibilities of phantom and levitation tricks. I discovered, for instance, how to produce a ghost of myself, and talk to it, and make it hold conversations with me.

This caused somewhat of a sensation on the stage when I first presented it ; and other phantom illusions did the same.

The best levitation trick, despite years of patient study and experiment, continued to be the one invented by my father, in which a girl walks on to the stage, is apparently hypnotized by the magician, lies down in a stone coffin, and then rises from it horizontally, and absolutely without any means of support, at a word of command from the "hypnotist".

I was doing this trick one day at St. George's Hall when a very small girl in the audience—I think she might have been about five years old—not merely "stole my thunder", but took the attention of the audience to such an extent, and this at the very climax of this thrilling trick, that it was not worth my while to finish it.

My assistant had come on the stage, been apparently hypnotized, lain down in the coffin, and had risen into the air from it, a long sash hanging meanwhile from her waist to the ground. Of course, the audience thought that the sash concealed a pillar or some such apparatus to raise her, and I obtained a little extra effect by twitching the sash away while she lay suspended about five feet from the stage, and showing that nothing had been hidden beneath it.

Then I advanced towards her motionless sleeping figure with a big steel hoop in my hand. This hoop had previously been examined by the audience, and passed as an unbroken ring of steel. My idea was to pass the steel hoop round the body of my levitated assistant, and move it along from her feet to her head, to show the audience that she was definitely not supported in any way whatever.

As I did this, in order to increase the effect, the orchestra, which had been playing mysterious Eastern music, suddenly stopped, leaving a period of absolute silence in which I was to develop the climax of my illusion.

I began to pass the hoop along, slowly and effectively. Then the silence, which felt almost a solid thing after the previous music, was cut as if by a knife.

"Mummy!" wailed an innocent childish voice, distinctly audible all over the theatre. "Mummy! I *can't* wait any longer. I can't really! I really *do* want to go this time!"

I am sorry to say that my assistant, despite the fact that she was suspended in mid-air in an hypnotic trance, giggled audibly. But it did not matter; indeed, I am afraid I laughed myself.

Any sounds from the stage were drowned in a roll of laughter that ran all over the theatre, from the floor to the roof. My illusion was forgotten; in fact, we finished it off as swiftly as possible and brought down the curtain, while the orchestra, at a nod from me, crashed into a triumphal march, to the strains of which the little girl and her mummy "went" like warriors walking to receive their laurels!

A night or two after this affair, again while we had a show in full swing but at a time when I was not actually on the stage myself, the head fly-man came rushing to me where I stood in the wings.

"My God, Mr. Jasper!" he gasped. "Your grandfather's standing up in the flies there!"

It was a startling announcement, naturally, since my grandfather had been dead nearly ten years. Yet the man's white face showed that he had received some sort of shock. I asked him to take me up to the place where he had seen the figure, but he point-blank refused to do so.

With a performance going on and myself due on the stage in about five minutes, I was in no mood to stand for too much imagination. Besides, I needed the man up there, to see to the curtain changes during the rest of the performance.

"Come on upstairs and show me what you saw, or else go and get your pay and clear out for good !" I snapped at him. "You needn't go too near whatever it is you saw. I'll do that. Just point out the place to me, that's all. Anyway, my grandfather never did anyone any harm."

The man was an old hand who had known J. N., and, like all his servants, worshipped the very ground he trod on. He muttered something, and ran ahead of me up the ladders into the flies, forty feet or so above the stage.

"There !" he quivered, pointing a shaking finger.

I got the shock of my life. We were standing directly above the footlights. The fly-rails ran round the outside of the dome, above the sides of the stage and round at the back. Standing at the point opposite us, against the back wall of the theatre, about forty feet above the stage, his arm on the fly-rail, and apparently intently watching the unconscious actors on the boards far below, was the figure of a man in full evening dress—undoubtedly the figure of my grandfather ! Through the forest of ropes that intervened, I could see his characteristic pose and his absorbed face.

"Wait here and tell me—signal to me if your voice might be heard in the theatre—when I get near the place where he is standing," I muttered. "I'm positive the thing's some sort of optical illusion."

I walked swiftly round the fly-rails to the spot where I had seen the figure standing, but there was nothing there. The fly-man gestured me to one side, and I took a couple of paces that way. Then he nodded, and his amazed and shocked face told its own story.

I went back to him and asked him what he had seen.

Without speaking, he jabbed a thumb towards the place I had just left. Standing there, still intently watching the stage, was the figure in evening dress.

"You—you walked—right through him, Mr. Jasper !" the flyman whispered.

Now here is a strange thing. That figure appeared there always at the moment the house-lights were turned up preceding a performance on the stage below. It stayed till the end of the performance ; when the lights went out, it vanished.

It was pretty obviously some extraordinary illusion—far more amazing than anything we did on the stage—caused by the lights shining through the network of ropes up there in the flies.

If one went round to the spot where the figure stood, nothing was visible. Yet a watcher stationed over the foot-lights could still see the brooding figure, and from that position it looked as if any investigator, passing round the back of the fly-rails, walked straight through the phantom as it leaned there staring down at the stage.

That curious impression remained in its place, quietly watching right through every performance, until Maskelyne's Theatre was sold to the B.B.C. Then they did all sorts of alterations and improvements, and apparently the particular combination of lighting and shadow was spoiled. I was broadcasting from St. George's Hall some months ago, and I went up into the flies to see if the ghostly figure of J. N. Maskelyne still kept his quiet ward. But he was gone.

Perhaps it was just as well, for none of the fly-men cared to go up along the back of the fly-rails after our discovery, and for the matter of that few of the artistes would do so either.

Throughout my first year as the controlling force on the

stage at St. George's Hall, after my father's death, I was constantly getting into awkward little situations and having to extricate myself, and generally finding out all the snags of managing a magic show.

I remember a particularly awkward moment that occurred one evening when I was giving an extra-special performance (they always *do* occur then !) before some C.I.D. inspectors, who had been sent tickets in acknowledgment of a little mystery they had cleared up in connection with some cash of ours which was doing the vanishing-trick nightly from the theatre takings.

Now, of all onlookers, I dread detectives most. Their training leads them to logical speculation on the way my tricks are done; they reject the obvious impossibilities which the magician flaunts as red herrings before the general audience, and are very apt to puzzle out the works of a trick if they are given the slightest clue.

You can judge my exasperation, therefore, when, in one of the big illusions that evening, I failed to get the cue which should have told me that my girl assistant had successfully secreted herself inside a complicated bit of apparatus off-stage, ready for the climax of my trick.

I made up some lines and waited for the cue, but it did not come. We had practised that trick for six months; in the event, it ran only four weeks, and was then withdrawn; but at the time I did not suppose that anything could possibly have gone wrong with it.

Finally, finding that my cue still did not come, I made an excuse to move near the side-curtains where I saw the girl standing beside the apparatus, looking frightened.

"Why aren't you inside ?" I asked, out of the corner of my mouth, while still keeping my face to the audience and apparently busying myself with the preparation of some other material on the stage.

"I've forgotten how," she answered tearfully.

I murmured some key directions, and next moment she was inside, I got my cue, and the trick proceeded smoothly to its conclusion.

After the show I asked the detectives if they had spotted the "works" of any of my tricks. But, thank goodness, they were as mystified as all the rest of the audience, and that is saying a good deal !

I have often been asked whether my apparatus on the stage costs me very much to construct. Well, some of it does, of course. I have one apparatus that cost me over £350 to build and patent, and yet the trick it performs only takes four minutes on the stage. But it is a good trick.

For three years I was the only performer of this trick in the world. Then I heard that a certain famous contemporary, an American who was then visiting England, had reproduced it, or even improved upon it a little. I went to see one of his shows.

Yes, he had produced my trick, and obtained just as good an effect as I did. But instead of spending £350 on his apparatus, he achieved the same effect by employing three men, placed at different angles, to pull simultaneously on little bits of string.

We live and learn !

For a good number of my most spectacular illusions I use—not complicated electric apparatus, as everyone supposes—but the good old gramophone motor. I have some hundreds of these motors in my workshops.

They have amazing strength ; they never break down ; and they are silent.

Black velvet, and to a lesser degree mirrors, play a very important part in the staging of some of my biggest illusions. Long before the art of camouflage by colours sprang into prominence during the Great War, we magicians had exploited it to a degree that would fill a layman with wonder.

Cobbler's wax, little steel springs and clips, and a profound knowledge of the more out-of-the-way tricks that the force of gravity can be persuaded to perform, are further items in a modern magician's box of tricks.

But most of all it is blarney—the fine art of making the onlooker think the wrong thing, hear the wrong thing and see the wrong thing. I wonder, now, just why there are no world-famous Irish illusionists?

CHAPTER XV

Dispatch-riding in the General Strike—Attacked by my colleagues—
Midsummer marriage—Nearly drowned in Beer—Children on
the stage—A magic competition at "Maskelynes"—Magicians
in trouble.

NINETEEN HUNDRED AND TWENTY-SIX seems to have been
an eventful year for me! Not the least of my adventures
were concerned with the General Strike.

Like, I suppose, the greater part of the rest of England's
population, I was not very greatly perturbed by events
during the first couple of days of the strike. I was rather
amused at the amazing variety of vehicles one saw in the
streets; old crock cars, ponies and traps, push-bikes,
equestrians' gee-gees, and once even a penny-farthing
bicycle that I saw swiftly ridden down Langham Place into
Regent Street.

But for me it was "business as usual"; audiences were
smaller, but what they lacked in numbers they made up in
enthusiasm.

On the third day of the stoppage, however, I was told
by an eye-witness how a tram-driver had been murdered by
his own mates. The man had been pulled from his tram, on
which he was working in spite of Union orders, and his
head kicked in, accidentally or deliberately. While being
hauled from his platform by brutal, willing hands, the man
screamed for mercy, shouting that he had been forced to
work because he could not otherwise find food for his wife
and children. The tram was rolled over on its side and
burned, and my informant, who had been a passenger, escaped with nothing more dangerous than abuse and jostling.

Something in that story made me see red. If that was the spirit of the strikers, then I for one would throw myself into the struggle to break their power.

By a bit of luck, we happened just previously to have given some passes to a special show at the Hall to some C.I.D. men, and one of these was able to get me a job as motor-cycle dispatch rider attached to Walham Green Police Station. This promised excitement, and I got it, though hardly of the type I had expected.

They gave me a very old, very crotchety motor-bike, which I learned was popularly called Jezebel—for obvious reasons. They also gave me a straw paliasse in the corner of a garage as sleeping accommodation, for my job necessitated that I should be available for duty twenty-four hours out of the twenty-four.

Most days I was given a hundred or so letters, in plain envelopes, and told to deliver them to a list of addresses that was rendered to me separately. The envelopes were identified only by numbers marked on them. They bore no addresses, and their contents were as often as not in code, in case they fell into the hands of strikers, I suppose.

I delivered them, according to instructions, at the most queer assortment of addresses. Some went to Scotland Yard; some went to other police-stations, and to the temporary police headquarters such as Hyde Park. But a good many were for obscure addresses ranging from Putney back-streets and Tottenham pubs to Belgrave Square mansions and Thames Ditton bungalows.

I have always wondered what was the secret behind the immense network of communications that the police and detective services kept up during the strike. Were they obtaining information? Were they laying plans in case the strike developed into civil war?

I cannot tell. But obviously there was something pretty

big in the way of organization going on, and only the controlling brains knew enough about it to be able to co-ordinate the whole into a logical plan of campaign.

As for me, I was just one of the units whose lot was "not to reason why". Often I used to bestride Jezebel at midnight, stutter and roar up to some address, steering by my mount's inadequate and blinking lights, deliver a letter, ride off to a place ten miles distant and deliver another, and then find that a third should have been handed in only a few hundred yards from the place where I had left the first. I was never given any guide as to districts, and, of course, street-names in unknown neighbourhoods conveyed very little to me.

Anyway, we muddled through!

Once my journeyings took me along the Kingston By-Pass Road. I was warned by the detectives at Walham Green that there was trouble in that direction, so I strapped on to my belt, outside my jacket, a huge service revolver of my brother's. I had no ammunition for it, and no licence either, for that matter, but it looked really good stuff!

Incidentally, I had no uniform, unless you can call an official armlet a uniform, and my police weapons were comprised solely of a stout truncheon, which I was forbidden by my superiors, almost on pain of death, ever to draw or even to display.

Near Kingston I found the road blocked by a crowd of excited men, who were in the act of burning a big black saloon car, the owner of which stood by in the grip of a couple of roughs. I rode up to them, pulled Jezebel up on her haunches—to which indignity she replied with a deafening squeal of brakes—and told the men to let their prisoner go.

They took one look at my artillery, and complied.

The gentleman then jumped on my pillion and we roared away before the main body of the destroyers quite knew what had happened. For a couple of miles I could hear the man behind me saying to himself : "Why couldn't they have left me Dolly's letters ! I don't care about the car, but why couldn't they have left me my letters !"

I have no idea whether Dolly was his wife or sweetheart or daughter, but the car was in the thousand-pound class, by the look of it. When I set him down and said good-bye, he was so absorbed in his lost letters that he almost forgot to thank me for the lift.

I returned by the same road an hour later, and the car was a gutted, twisted ruin.

About three days before the strike ended I was sent with an urgent message from Walham Green to Scotland Yard, in the early hours of the morning. I was thundering along as usual at about fifty miles an hour, for Jezebel was a fast hussy when she was not mulish, and the empty streets exhilarated me so much that I was singing at the top of my voice as I rode.

Near Victoria Station I was going over a cross-roads when, without warning, a big Daimler shot out of a side-turning, loomed gigantic over me, and crashed me broadside on across its radiator. It executed a skid like an outsize ballet-girl, I went flying, and hit a street-island with my hip. The island preserved a stolid demeanour, Jezebel bounced off and roared her tale of woe to the night skies, and the next thing I knew was that a number of men were solicitously bending over me and asking each other if I was dead. I soon convinced them about that !

What annoyed me most was that I had been knocked flying by a car-load of *detectives* ! Why they were in such a hurry I have no idea ; but it did seem hard to be knocked out by one's own colleagues after braving the worst terrors of the strikers.

Not that the strikers were really very terrible. Indeed,

whenever I lost myself delivering dispatches, as I did half a dozen times a day, I had to depend on them entirely to find myself for me. And on one occasion a kindly group picketing a factory gave me scalding black tea and bread and cheese because they said I looked cold.

After my accident I ceased working for the mechanized section of our detective organization, largely because Jezebel had deposited a good portion of her entrails on the pavement near Victoria. Whether, as in the case of her famous predecessor of the same name, the dogs ate them, I cannot say, but doubt it because my Jezebel was so very old and tough.

As a new interest, I supervised for a short time the formation of a local branch of mounted Special Constables. I had suggested this idea on my enrolment, as I was a good rider myself, but it was postponed, like a great many other useful proposals, till the strike was over before it was put into effect.

An even more bitter instance of this sort of thing, to my fevered imagination, was that, though I had besought the authorities, both local and headquarters, all through the strike, for relief dispatch riders, and for something better than mouldy straw to sleep on, nothing was heard of any result to my appeals until the day the strike ended.

On that very morning, some proper hair mattresses and warm blankets arrived, together with a squadron of half a dozen fresh-faced motor-cyclists who had been told to put themselves at my disposal.

Think of it! Had I been luckier, I could have reposed on my mattress all day and issued lordly orders to the underlings. As it was, I worked single-handed till there was no more work to do, and then they insulted me with all I had previously sought. Who'd be a patriot!

My hip was not permanently damaged by my accident,

but I found that it gave me trouble afterwards at odd times.

On Midsummer Day, 1926, I was married to Miss Home-Douglas. According to all authorities, Midsummer Day is an occasion of great magic, and I certainly had true magician's luck in the choice of the girl who has ever since been my greatest inspiration, and to whom any success I may since have achieved has been mainly due.

We spent our honeymoon at Beer, on the Devon coast. I was out swimming there, one glorious summer morning, when my damaged hip, which had been treacherously well-behaved for the past weeks, suddenly gave way. The pain was intense, and I sank down through the water, despite convulsive efforts to keep my head above the surface.

It just shows you how lucky I was to marry on Mid-summer Day, for my wife was watching me from the shore, and saw me threshing the water in my struggles. She became alarmed, and shouted urgently to an old fisherman who was out in his boat attending to some crab-pots a hundred yards to my left.

The old mariner looked up, saw my head disappear, drove his boat to the spot with a few powerful strokes, and plunged overside to search for me. It was lucky for me; I had ceased to struggle, and was floating about in the cold green depths in a sort of contented torpor. He dragged me to the surface, got me into his boat, and took me to the shore.

I was rather wet inside and out, but no serious damage had been done. The amazing thing was that, though I made what very inadequate acknowledgment I could, since the man had probably saved my life, he was infinitely more delighted with the little magic show I gave later to amuse his children and some other youngsters who had gathered for the occasion.

Children are undoubtedly the magician's best audience. They accept him so very whole-heartedly ; they have explanations for a good many of his tricks (quite wrong ones), but they still give him full marks if he amuses them. They are so delightfully free from the *blasé*.

I once had fifty children on the stage with me at once, at a children's matinée we were giving at St. George's Hall. I had to "do my stuff" under their eyes, and of course they are very sharp-eyed when they choose.

One of the small girls—a lady of perhaps seven or eight years old—desperately wanted to talk to me about weddings. She asked me if I had ever been to a wedding, and was thrilled to learn that I had recently attended my own. We talked and talked while I got on with my illusions, but she would not be satisfied.

Eventually I had to sit down on the stage with her, the rest of the youngsters squatting round in an admiring circle, and get this wedding palaver properly settled before I could finish my tricks.

One of the most exciting experiences I ever had with children occurred at about this time. We held a nation-wide competition at St. George's Hall for young conjurers, and although no tricks actually new to me were given, some of the presentations of them were quite novel and exceedingly attractive.

A "Miss Paula" of Hastings, who could not have been more than thirteen, opened proceedings with a clever trick. She laid three handkerchiefs loosely on a table ; and on another table she placed three handkerchiefs knotted end to end. The tables were about ten feet apart, and both were under the eyes of the audience the whole time.

At a wave of the hand, the knotted handkerchiefs undid themselves and the others became knotted.

When I add that the audience, which was an "invitation"

one, consisted entirely of famous magicians, most of them members of the Magic Circle itself, and that they could not actually see how this trick was performed, though probably they guessed, it says volumes for the young conjurer.

Lawrence Lewis made billiard balls appear and disappear from between his outspread fingers, and anyone who has tried tricks with ivories will bear me out that they are a pretty difficult medium for magic. Thimbles appeared and vanished from the tips of his fingers at a word of command, though he did not apparently move his hands or bend the digits at all.

Robin Hood, a boy of under twelve, materialized a laurel chaplet for himself out of thin air while bowing to the applause that greeted his appearance on the stage—a most appropriate and effective illusion. Then he held up a playing-card, shook it, and it became a size smaller, and repeated this trick till the card had diminished to the size of a finger-nail while never actually disappearing for one moment from the gaze of the onlookers.

This boy was gifted with exceptional hands, and already had a good knowledge of how to use them, making them do the entertaining instead of using his voice too much—a usual fault with beginners.

Since those days, Robin, and his father and mother, have become three of our dearest friends.

I have to thank magic for introducing me to many such splendid friends up and down the country.

Robin now has his own little stage fitted up in the drawing-room at home, with footlights, spotlights, scenery —in fact, everything possible to help him to present a perfect performance. Despite his youth, he is one of the best magicians I have ever seen, and it is a great shame that there is really no need for him to become a professional. Magic is simply his hobby.

I have spent many hours with him, trying out new big illusions on a small scale. I have also made him apparatus for a good number of tricks that I myself perform on the stage.

It is, of course, very often vitally necessary to give new illusions a trial run in reduced form, since apparatus is often exceedingly costly to construct, and one wants to polish up and become perfect first, before building the final copy for professional use. The fact that I have been able to try ideas out thus has often saved me a great deal of expense and resulted in a better trick in the end.

Robin has recently left Eton, having gone a very long way since I first met him on Maskelynes' stage, but I still see a great deal of him, and am delighted at his shrewd comments and suggestions whenever we try out an illusion together.

Last to take the stage in the St. George's Hall competition was a bare-kneed lad named Richard Barrs. He set up a blackboard near the footlights so that it was free from possible trap-doors, assistants and so on, and then commanded the words "Good night!" to appear on it.

In an instant, the chalked words materialized on the board, in round boyish writing. Then he commanded them to vanish again, which they promptly did.

He produced a dish of lemons and a pack of cards, apparently out of thin air. Then he handed down the dish to the interested professional magicians in the stalls, and one of them selected a lemon from it. Meanwhile another member of the audience chose a card at random from the pack, and returned it to the young illusionist.

The lemon was then cut open before our eyes, and the selected card was found rolled up in the middle of the lemon.

This boy, Richard Barrs, won the premier award as a

juvenile male magician, with Robin Hood second; and Paula led the girls' side. She received a huge box of magic apparatus from Hamleys, and Barrs was given a ten-pound note and Robin a cheque. In addition, the two winners appeared, by special arrangement, for a single performance on the St. George's Hall stage on the following Saturday afternoon, at one of our public shows.

As was perhaps only natural, some of these very promising amateurs fumbled a trick or two during the competition, but the show on the whole was a marvellous success and gave great enjoyment to all us old hands who looked on.

Even those who made mistakes need not have been downcast. Real magicians make mistakes, too, sometimes.

I well remember a substitute performer at St. George's Hall, when I was a small boy, who not only made a slip, but committed the very much graver crime of not knowing what to do when he had made it.

An illusion called the Phantom Dancer was being presented, in which the magician was supposed to waltz round the stage with a girl assistant who vanished from his arms as a clock on the stage struck midnight—rather untruthfully, I fear!

On the occasion of which I am writing, something went wrong, the illusionist lost his head instead of the lady, and started wrestling with her—or so it seemed—in the absurd hope of forcing the apparatus to work. Boos, hisses, cat-calls and advice brought the curtain down with a run, not only on that disastrous performance, but on the magician's reputation.

On another occasion, a clever disappearing trick was being carried out with a hen. An obstinate, clucking old fowl is not an easy "assistant" at the best of times, and usually this illusion, which consisted of "vanishing" the hen from a covered coop on a table, and making her appear in a hitherto empty coop on a distant table, was a very popular one.

This time it was more popular than ever before, but hardly in the way intended. The conjurer "vanished" his hen, withdrew the cloth with a flourish from the empty coop, walked over to the second table, confidently uncovered the coop there—when lo! a fine young cockerel stretched himself within and crowed lustily.

Hardly had the audience ceased to giggle than the young man behind the scenes who had been responsible for this remarkable transformation was on his way to the stage-door with, in his pocket, a week's salary in lieu of notice.

Last year, a small boy, whose father I knew, asked me to teach him some minor conjuring tricks with which to impress his schoolmates on his return to durance after the holidays.

I showed him some small tricks, and he proved a remarkably apt pupil. A week later I received a pained letter from the lad's mother.

It appeared that he had been to church parade with the family the previous Sunday, and when a solemn sidesman had come round with the bag, my pupil had created a local sensation by holding out his penny, making it vanish from before the very eyes of the onlookers, slowly and dramatically producing it from the sidesman's beard, and then placing the coin in the bag. The effect on the youth's small sister had, I was told, been peculiarly demoralizing.

He had stoutly refused to tell anyone where he had learned the trick, but my fame as a conjurer and my regrettable good nature were well known to his parents, and they drew the cruel conclusion that I had not only taught him the trick, but suggested the idea for staging it so notably. Which was, of course, a sheer libel.

Indeed, it is not all fun being a magician! Not long ago I was amusing some friends at home by showing them a trick whereby I filled a glass of water to the brim, put a sheet of cardboard over it, turned the lot upside down on the oak dining-table, and withdrew the cardboard, finally sliding the glass to the edge of the table and pouring the water into a jug there without spilling a drop.

This trick, of course, marks the table, but oak is capable of being well polished so that the blemish can be removed entirely.

While I was in the middle of this little trick, my small son came in to say good night, and begged to be allowed to see me finish my effort before he went to bed. As usual, I was weak with him and said yes.

One morning later, he came to me in a great state of excitement.

"Daddy!" he announced triumphantly, "I've been doing your trick with the glass of water. I've turned it upsydown, but now I'm 'fraid to get it off. Will _you_ come and finish it for me?"

How, short of an absolute miracle, the child had done it, I cannot pretend to explain, but he had got as far as reversing the glass and withdrawing the cardboard, and only a drop or two of water had escaped.

But the trouble was that he had operated on a little Queen Anne inlaid walnut table of considerable value; the stain, of course, will take years of patient polishing to remove from the veneer, and will leave a permanent mark on the inlaid work.

I think that the worst of all my trials as a professional magician occurred a year or two ago. I was "vanishing" a lady from a box, before a packed and distinguished audience. They did not see her go, but I watched the lady disappear safely into the wings, opened the box—and she was still there !

I begged the audience to keep their seats, and promised to do the trick over again. This time there was no mistake ; I watched the lady go into the wings, waited for my cue, showing that she was safely out of the way, and dramatically threw up the lid of the box.

There she was, still within !

And then I woke up ! It was about time ! I was sweating as if I had run a fast race ; and I had been gnawing my lip hard.

For about six months I was hag-ridden by that dream. I could hardly ever sleep right though a night without it. It made me uncomfortable and worried lest I should really do this silly thing on the stage.

One day, in desperation, I did it deliberately at rehearsal, arranging with my assistant to stay in the box. Everyone laughed, and I could not help joining in. After that, the dream never returned.

CHAPTER XVI

AFTER twelve months accustoming myself to my new work as controlling force at St. George's Hall, I managed to get things running on a routine that I understood and could adequately control.

I met with many difficulties and made a few mistakes. But I enjoyed every minute of the work, even though it made almost superhuman demands on my time.

In order to keep the profits up to a standard level, I had to do a good many things besides making magic on the stage. There was the task of superintending the work in the shops where our apparatus was made ; the arranging and changing of programmes ; the engagement of new artistes ; the matter of advertisements ; and even then hundreds of odd jobs were waiting for me to do them.

For instance, in 1928, I turned decorator on a big scale, to meet an emergency.

The fact was that St. George's Hall terribly needed painting. It was thoroughly dirty inside, and in places the plaster had broken away from walls and ceiling, leaving hideous rents. The trouble, from our point of view, was that redecorating at that time was a very expensive job.

We got several estimates from London decorating firms. The best one asked a price of £282, and proposed to keep the theatre closed down only three weeks. Nor was this particularly unreasonable ; the job was a big one, for the

theatre measures fifty-nine feet internally from the floor
to the top of the dome.

But three weeks' loss of business, plus £282, meant a
good deal more than we were prepared to spend. At 'a
rather agitated directors' meeting I put forward a counter-
suggestion.

"I'll do it for you !" I announced, with some pride.

"You must be a better magician even than we thought
you !" replied someone rather unkindly.

But I did not propose to do it by magic. On the contrary, I had all my plans cut and dried ; and, in the end,
I won the rest of the meeting over to my way of thinking.

"I don't see how he can make it any *worse* than it is
now," laughed one of my critics. "And he *may* make it
better, with a bit of luck."

I went off straight away and borrowed a 55-foot ladder,
which was carried through the streets to the theatre with
myself proudly marching along in front.

I engaged two volunteer assistants, bought about
fifteen gallons of grey paint, one gallon of gold paint,
three or four dozen brushes of all shapes and sizes, some
overalls, and a very doggish-looking cap. I hired a big
electric spray, laid in several hundred cigarettes, and then
really got going.

> Slap-dab, slap-dab, up and down the brickwork,
> Slap-dab all day long . . .

as the classic says. And, after it, a lightning change out of
my overalls and cap (which soon became armour-plated
with paint !) into faultless evening dress, and on to the
stage for my two or three performances, after which I fell
asleep from sheer fatigue, only to be up with the lark in
the morning, and away up my long ladder to begin afresh
my slap-dab task.

We kept the theatre open the whole time ; the job took us only twelve days instead of the three weeks dubiously considered sufficient by the professionals ; and the cost was between £30 and £40 instead of over £280.

It makes "man's time" look a pretty big item in decorating charges, doesn't it ?

We did make a few mistakes, of course, because we were so very enthusiastic, and the record time we were making over the job went to our heads. But the place looked very creditable when we had done.

Nor is this merely the opinion of a proud artist inclined to consider his own goose a spotless swan. For when I was in St. George's Hall some months ago, I noticed with interest that it had not been repainted since I did the job. There were my mistakes, as large as life, still visible to my critical eyes ; and, what was more, beautiful grey-and-gold upholstered seating and appointments had been fitted throughout the theatre.

Since my work had thus obviously received the austere approval of those arbiters of elegance, the Uncles and Aunties of the B.B.C., I think mere words of mine become superfluous ! Ses you, Twins !

It was just after joining the Painters' and Decorators' Union that I made my first film. It was a rather astounding effort.

In it I played the part of the detective hero who discovered a thief among some guests at an hotel. I then abandoned all the best Scotland Yard and Sherlock Holmes methods, and, instead, made the robber return the jewels by frightening him with various terrifying illusions.

The picture was called "Room 19", but it was never shown. I have still got a complete reel of it, and I am saving it up till my boy is twenty-one, when I shall show it at his birthday party. I think it should prove one of the best turns of the evening, though perhaps by that time it will seem to contain more comedy than drama.

My second film, "Kidnapped", was a much better effort, and had a much more plausible story.

In it a famous magician offers to give £10,000 to a committee, selected from the audience, if he is unable to perform a certain trick. This consists in sealing and roping an empty chest, and, when it is opened twenty-four hours later, producing a girl from it.

Crooks learn of the challenge, get themselves selected as the committee, and kidnap the girl. The magician follows, tries to rescue the girl, fails, and is forced at revolver-point to open the box on the stage.

Aha ! The girl is inside after all, her escape having been effected, by another bit of magic, just in time to allow her to complete the trick.

The box-trick employed in this film was the old original box-trick which my grandfather used in his magical sketch, "Will, the Witch and the Watchman".

This was the very last silent film made in Great Britain. It was sent to America to be fitted with sound ; and it had a successful run both as a silent and as a talkie film. Indeed, quite recently I saw it advertised at a big cinema in the East End of London.

I found my first experiences of film work very interesting. The job is exacting, and totally different from the sort of thing one does on the stage. To the beginner, it is almost uncanny to have to act without audience, orchestra, effects or footlights, and without the comfortable atmosphere of the theatre. A few camera-men and directors, a "set" as small as can possibly be used, showing perhaps a small section of a room or the front or back of a car, the dead silence that was necessary when making a non-talking picture—these things were disconcerting in the extreme.

Sometimes, indeed, the yellow-painted faces of the actors, showing ghastly in the sweep of the arclights, give quite a good impression of another world altogether.

Nor is magic easy to reproduce for film work. On the stage the magician blarneys his way to fame. He contrives, by a word or a gesture, to take the attention of the audience from the things they shouldn't see. You can't do that with the camera.

It was during the time when I was making my second film that I received a curious and horrible reminder that this modern world of talkies and radio and electricity and aeroplanes has not yet shaken off all the terrors that beset our superstitious forefathers of primitive times.

One of our magicians at St. George's Hall, a veteran who had appeared there in my grandfather's day, but had been working on his own for many years and had later returned to us, had a breakdown on the stage while he was performing an illusion before the audience.

It was stated in the newspapers at the time that his health had given way, and that he was to take a spell of rest. A fortnight later his suicide "while of unsound mind" was reported.

Everyone thought that it was a case of overwork and nervous breakdown. On the contrary, that man was frightened to death.

I knew the inside story at the time, but I would not tell it, partly because its publication might have had serious consequences then, and partly because the dead man had still one living relative. That lady has since died, and now there is no one of the family left to grieve, even if they could identify the principal of my tale.

When the illusionist failed to perform his trick on the stage, and then broke down in tears, the curtain came down, and I interviewed him behind the scenes. I was shocked to see that his hands were shaking, and that the pupils of his eyes were enormous, so that the whites had disappeared, giving him a dreadful appearance.

I thought he had been taking drugs, but he poured out his whole story, and it was not at all what I had expected.

He said that, some months earlier, he had been introduced to a sect of Devil-worshippers in London. He had always scoffed at such things, and had supposed that they were simply a band of highly strung people who dabbled in ancient magic, and who had persuaded themselves into believing it of supernatural origin. He joined the sect in the hope of learning some new tricks to use on the stage.

If ever a man was a martyr to his art, that illusionist was the one!

After a few innocuous ceremonies, at which, nevertheless, some tricks were produced that were quite new to the novice, it was explained to him that he would have to be "sealed to the Devil" before he could be initiated into the deeper mysteries. Since he had long ago abandoned the idea of a personal Devil as a childish superstition, he had no objection.

He then attended a Witches' Sabbath at which, according to his account, filthy blasphemies took place which cannot be described in a decent book. He had wanted to escape, but some power greater than his own simply prevented his feet from moving.

In the end, in a climax of abomination at which he drank warm blood and permitted one of his veins to be opened, he was "sealed to the Devil".

He said that the Satanists had explained to him that he would now become swiftly rich and powerful, so long as he sustained his allegiance to his evil Master, and so long as he never uttered a word to any outsider about the Devil-worship and its devotees. He had been warned, however, that the breaking of either commandment would mean his own death.

At this point in his story he whimpered that he wanted to commit suicide, but was terrified of what would happen to his soul afterwards. He also said that he had been dabbling on the Stock Exchange, though he had no knowledge whatever of markets, and that he had become rich through amazing rises in stock he had bought. This he attributed to occult influence, but a more mundane explanation was that he had acted on the advice of a certain very famous banker who was a member of the evil circle.

Naturally enough, I thought that the whole story was simply the phantasm of a fevered mind. I told the magician that he must have a spell of absolute rest, and asked him if he would go abroad for a few weeks, at the theatre's expense.

But the man was full of his Diabolism story. He said he had to attend another Witches' Sabbath at the house of a woman society leader in Mayfair in a week's time, and that it was more than his life was worth to be absent from it. However, he promised to try to get leave of absence, and to go abroad if he succeeded in doing so.

On the morning after this Satanist meeting I called at my unhappy friend's address in Camden Town and went up to his rooms.

I tapped on the door, but received no reply; so, as I had often been there before, I walked in, meaning to wait for him. I got a shock.

The man himself lay taut and outstretched on the floor, his eyes wide open, his face paper-white, looking as if he were in a cataleptic fit.

I ran to him, loosened his collar, and splashed cold water from the bathroom onto his face. Suddenly he sat up stiffly, but for some minutes he could not speak.

Then he stammered out an incredible story. He said he had attended the meeting in Mayfair, and that several people of national reputation had been there, including the banker, a famous film actress and two leading financiers.

Behind closed doors they had repeated the Lord's Prayer backwards, cut the throats of some doves and dabbled in the blood, repeated Arabic charms and chants, and committed all sorts of abominations. Finally, at some spell more potent than the rest, the figure of a little black man in a black silk cloak had suddenly appeared among them. He emitted a stench like a decaying corpse; and he touched each worshipper in turn.

When he touched my magician friend, the latter lost consciousness. When he recovered I was bending over him in his own flat.

The man was so obviously very ill that I simply forced him to accompany me to my own doctor, whom I privately asked to examine him for signs of narcotics, and to warn him that he must get right away from London for a rest and change.

"Well," said the doctor later, while the patient was in another room getting his things on again, "I warned him for you, Jasper. But what's the man been doing? There's no trace whatever of drugs or alcohol; he's had some ghastly shock. I've told him straight out that unless he goes into a nursing-home at once I won't be responsible for him. He's sane enough, but something's gone pretty badly wrong with him."

When the illusionist rejoined us, the doctor and I both tried all we knew to persuade him to go straight into a nursing-home. This he flatly refused to do until a week later. Nothing we could say would make him change his mind.

Later, in a taxi, he told me his reasons.

"There is just one more meeting that I must attend," he stammered. "We're meeting at a house on Barnes Common next Friday night. After that, I'll go abroad if you like. *He* has said I shall be released after this meeting."

The poor fellow was in no fit state to attend any more of these infernal séances. I could not persuade him to stay away, but in the end, after cruel badgering, I forced the address of the meeting-place out of him, and decided to attend it myself, to try to protect him.

I went over the ground beforehand, and on the Friday night, as soon as it was dark, I slipped swiftly over a fence into the grounds of a big house on the edge of Barnes Common. I made my way to the side of a large double garage, where the ceremony was to take place, and hid in a clump of laurels against the wall.

Then, with great care, and using a hammer padded with cloth, I drove a nail through the cement between the bricks, and withdrew it, thus giving myself a peephole which commanded a restricted view of the interior.

Just before midnight a party of a dozen men and women came furtively into the garage and locked the doors. One lighted some black candles at the far end.

In the faint illumination, I got my first view of the place. A black-marble block stood at the end of the interior. It was draped with black curtains, beautifully worked with embroidery showing various beastly manifestations of the Devil, and the designs were such that, in their uncanny power, they suggested the work of a mad artist.

On the walls nearby were paintings of an abominable nature showing men, women and children in the grasp of a horrible little deformed black man in a black suit.

The first thing I ascertained, after a lot of twisting about to get a view, was that my friend was not among the worshippers, for which I was heartily thankful.

They were all clad in white cloaks with black crosses on them. One, who seemed to be the leader, went up to the marble block and fished out from behind it a pig's-head mask, which he put on.

Then they all joined in a sort of hushed chorus in a language I could not understand. The masked man repeated responses, and uttered charms, and danced about. Presently he began foaming at the mouth. Then he dragged up from behind the marble altar a black cockerel, which screeched for a moment, till he cut short its protest by slashing open its throat.

At this point all the worshippers flung off their cloaks, stepping forward naked, and licking at the blood from the still-flapping bird.

I had seen more than enough. As my friend was not there my mission was abortive. I returned home, which I reached about two in the morning, and went to bed, fully determining that I would visit my friend first thing next—or rather that—day, and bully him into entering a good nursing-home, or taking a continental holiday. I thought my task would be easier because he had not attended the Devil's Mass at Barnes, since his absenting himself showed that he still possessed a remnant of courage.

I had an early breakfast, meaning to go round to Camden Town immediately I had finished. But while I was eating my bacon I read in my newspaper that my friend had been found, in the small hours of that morning, in his lodging, dead, with a gas-tube in his mouth.

That is the story of my only experience of Black Magic.

I wanted to go to the police, but what sort of a story had I? I should have been told to go and sleep it off. The suicide was recorded in the usual kindly way, as having taken place while the victim was unsound of mind. I wonder!

o

There is nothing much to add to the story, except a plea, from the very bottom of my soul, to all who ever feel tempted to dabble with Black Magic, to abstain from touching it. I profess to scoff at it myself; I do not believe that the Devil can be raised by human agency.

But this I know from my own experience. That minds can be unhinged and misery untold let loose by playing with the fire of Diabolism. I have talked this story over since with the doctor who examined my poor friend so shortly before his death, and he tells me that our asylums and prisons are fed every year with a shocking number of persons who have dabbled in Satanism and ended in madness or worse.

Not long ago a very famous detective, the last man in the world to let his imagination run riot, stated in print that Devil-worship was responsible for a large proportion of the crimes against very small children that take place annually. Certainly, any old book on the subject will confirm that child-murder is a vital tenet of the filthy creed.

Leave it alone ! To all those who value their reason I say again—leave it alone !

The trick which the illusionist was performing when he collapsed, and so began my connection with this Satanism affair, was one which I have often given myself. It is rather a good trick, and I once had a spontaneous and unintended suggestion for improving it.

A plate-glass case is wheeled on to the stage. The case is steel-bound, with a glass lid, kept down by four padlocks. It moves on castors and is raised by a framework nine inches clear of the stage, so that the audience can see beneath it.

A committee is invited up on to the stage to examine the glass case and pass it as empty and trick-proof. Then they padlock the lid down and keep the keys. At this point

I throw a cloth over the case, turn it completely round once on its castors to show the audience that the back is as solid as the front (though the committee who stand round all the time can see for themselves) pull the cloth off—and lo ! there is a girl inside !

At a matinée performance in 1929 I was about to perform this trick, and invited the committee as usual from the audience. Those know-alls who explain that these committees are always stage-hands in disguise will perhaps be shocked to learn that one member of this particular committee was more than a little inebriated when he stepped on to the stage. He even had the mouth of a substantial silver flask sticking out of his pocket at the time.

However, a magician can't start objecting to his committee, because then it *would* seem as if they were not expected to include genuine members of the audience. So I gave him a key, the box was examined, and the padlock fastened.

"I tell you what !" exclaimed my shaky friend at this point, in a voice of sepulchral solemnity. "I tell you all what. What ! Thash not glash. Ish no more a glash cashe'n I am. Get me, Steve ?"

The audience, to put it candidly, were delighted. When the committee-man advanced swiftly on the case and drew his flask from his pocket, they were more delighted still. It was only when he struck the case a tremendous wallop on the front, smashing the whole front panel into smithereens, that the general opinion seemed to be that he was going just a bit too far.

Well, of course, one had to do something. So I borrowed an early edition of an evening paper, that another committee-man was carying, and pasted it over the broken front of the case. Then I explained that, since the newspaper was there, I should not need a cloth.

I simply uttered the magic word "Abracadabra!" and a loud shout from the committee announced that the girl had materialized in that instant inside the damaged case. Incidentally, she cut her wrist on a bit of fallen glass inside there ; but that I did not discover till afterwards, when she declared that it was all in the day's work.

Of course, the trick was a huge success, and we even had a discussion behind the scenes as to whether it would not be worth while to break the panel at every performance. But as this plate class cost us £4 17s. per panel we couldn't make a commercial proposition of it, and had to abandon the idea.

Committees in conjuring are of all sorts. You find some members who want to get laughs for themselves, some who try to catch the illusionist out, some who are amateur conjurers trying to learn a trick or two—but the vast majority are decent people, only anxious to prevent obvious trickery, as it is their right to do, and with a keen sense of helping along the performance and adding to everyone's enjoyment.

I have had a lot of experience of all the various kinds, and I still prefer to do a trick which necessitates a committee, because it is almost always more fun that way. I owe my sincerest thanks to all the thousands of people who have helped me in this way up and down the British Isles.

But please—I *do* bar those who have dined not wisely but too well !

CHAPTER XVII

Off to South Africa with twelve tons of magic—Nature puts up a rival magic show—A Zulu witch-doctor puts a curse on me—A python round my neck—Three escapes from the Zulu's curse—I meet a poltergeist.

IN 1930, after having received several invitations, I decided to take a full-sized magic show on tour to South Africa.

The decision was a momentous one for me. In the first place, about forty years had elapsed since a Maskelyne show had left England. More important still, the tour that I planned necessitated carrying twelve tons of magic along with me!

For you must know that a company of illusionists necessarily take their apparatus from place to place as they travel. This is difficult enough in England, where railways and first-class motor-services reach out to every town and village, and where a journey of a couple of hundred miles between performances is about the worst that any week-end can threaten.

In South Africa, where the two hundred miles is turned into thousands and then multiplied, and where transport problems often have to be solved by bullock-waggons, or native porters who carry everything on their heads, twelve tons of fragile machinery becomes somewhat of a nightmare. To say nothing of the difficulty of transporting it all from England in the first place.

However, I did want to give the inhabitants of the Union a really first-class show, so in addition to the illusion apparatus, which was packed in forty-four vast crates, I selected a crack company to go with me, including Ling Foo, a Chinese magician, Ben Said, a fine Egyptian illusionist, Finlay Dunn with a splendid piano and burlesque turn, my sister Mary, my wife's sister Miss Cecil Home-Douglas, Glen Grafton, Alfred Barber as my manager and Walter Howell as stage-manager. Howell's father was my grandfather's master-carpenter for many years.

Our crates contained, in addition to the apparatus for over a hundred big illusions and tricks, some fifteen hundred pieces of music and a huge variety of special costumes.

We opened at the Empire, Johannesburg, before a public as enthusiastic as any to which I have ever played. We performed some dramatic disappearing tricks; I changed a jewelled decoration into a girl before the eyes of the audience; an "anti-gravity" globe slid up and down a steel rod, though with no apparent means of support; a fishing-line, swung from the stage, suddenly became weighted with a large goldfish while in full view of the onlookers; and I gave a variant of the old ribbon-from-a-hat trick by coming on the stage dressed as an American salesman and producing from my small attaché-case everything necessary to stock a reasonable-sized general store, even including a charming girl assistant.

The most appreciated turn of the lot, I think, was one in which I built a small canvas ark on the stage, showing each piece to the audience so that they should see that I was not deceiving them! Then, when the ark was placed in such a position that they could see above it, behind it, beneath it and all round it, I gave a dramatic representation of Noah coming into port, and produced from my ark sufficient animals to crowd the big stage.

While I was at Johannesburg I obtained permission to descend the world-famous Robinson Deep gold-mine.

Conditions in the great mining area south, east and west of the city more resemble those of a barracks than of a centre of industry. Regulations are extraordinarily strict ; no one is allowed to enter or leave the place without obtaining a countersigned pass ; and the district, whose buildings extend for over fifty miles, is heavily guarded by police.

Everything is covered with thick white dust from the ore-crushing operations, and the din of the stamps is so deafening that, after leaving the place, one cannot hear anything for half an hour or so.

The very greatest precautions are taken to prevent the Kaffir labourers from secreting any gold-dust about their persons and smuggling it out of the neighbourhood. It is said that much loss was caused formerly by their swallowing the dust in quantity, and later reproducing it by the aid of an emetic, but I cannot say if this is true or not.

On the whole I was surprised that the authorities allowed a magician into such a place. At one period they handed me a couple of gold bricks, worth £4000 apiece, which I managed to heave on to my shoulders and painfully balance there for the few moments necessary to have my photograph taken "as a really wealthy man".

If they had not been so terribly heavy, I should perhaps have been tempted to "vanish" those gold bricks !

From Johannesburg we passed on to Pretoria, Pietermaritzburg and Ladysmith. In the latter town my company met with a disconcerting reception. The audience, as always, was delightful ; but Dame Nature, evidently feeling that these human magicians were becoming presumptuous, showed us what *real* magic can be like.

Personally, I did not enjoy the experience !

Our show was nearing its close, after a very successful evening, when a sudden terrific crash of thunder sounded outside, and a veritable cloudburst of hail descended without warning on to the tin roof of the Town Hall where we were appearing. This hall was used as a hospital in the Boer War.

Hail in England is one thing; in South Africa it is sometimes quite another! Almost before I realized what it was that was causing the deafening clatter and rattle, a glass skylight directly above my head had been smashed by the storm, and lumps of ice fully as big as golf-balls came crashing down and bouncing as much as a foot high from the boards of the stage. I was told next day that several oxen, which were pasturing when the storm broke out and were unable to find shelter, were beaten to death by the falling ice.

At the time I was in the very midst of a decapitation trick. My assistant had been laid face downwards on an oak chest; I had covered his head with a cloth, apparently cut off the head, removed the cloth, walked round the stage showing it to the audience, and was just about to return to the decapitated body, whose shoulders were still bleeding, when the storm commenced.

This trick necessitates the assistant keeping absolutely motionless while his headless trunk is shown to the audience. But the jagged ice-lumps pouring through the broken skylight were crashing on to his back as he lay there, and one which hit me on the side of the head almost knocked me out, so I was frantic with anxiety for the still figure of the "decapitated" victim.

Faster than I have ever done in my life, I completed the trick, and my assistant and I ran off the stage. Personally I felt as if I had been clubbed several times on the head with some sharp instrument, and a trickle of blood was running into my left eye from a cut made by a huge hailstone on the edge of my forehead.

Several crates of our magic apparatus had been left in the passage outside the stage-door of the theatre. Afraid lest these should be damaged, I ran immediately to the stage-door, meaning to drag them under cover.

The door seemed stuck tight, but I forced it open with my shoulder. Then it would not close, for the weight had been caused by a veritable torrent, about nine inches deep, that was pouring along the passage outside. Before I could drag the door shut again this torrent had diverted a good part of itself down the steps into the back regions of the theatre, and I had to wade back to my dressing-room, after abandoning all hope of saving the crates outside, some of which I had seen floating away on the stream during my brief glimpse into the outer world.

Returned to the dressing-room again I found everything in awful disorder. I suppose the flood water must have been entering the theatre elsewhere as well ; at least, my room had about six inches of scummy water covering the floor, and an absolute plague of little green frogs had taken residence there, and were jumping about, in and out of open crates of illusion apparatus, on my dressing-table, on the clothes which I had discarded for my stage evening-dress—everywhere.

For the first time in my life I felt a deep sympathy with the Pharaoh of the Exodus who was similarly plagued !

Lifting what apparatus I could on to my dressing-table, chairs—anywhere out of the flood—I raced off again to rejoin my company, who were in sore trouble in the wings of the theatre. The stage was absolutely untenable, owing to the hail that still crashed steadily down through the broken skylight. What were we to do ?

After a hasty consultation I walked gingerly to a place by the footlights where the hail could not reach me, though lumps bounced malevolently at me from the middle of the stage.

"Ladies and gentlemen !" I shouted, making myself

heard above the din of the storm, "as you see, we cannot carry on from the stage. But we do not want to rob you of part of the show, and in any case you cannot very well leave the theatre till the weather improves a bit. My company proposes to carry on in the gangways of the theatre itself. It will be rather more difficult to produce our illusions surrounded by the audience in this way, so we must ask your indulgence for the tricks we show."

A tremendous outburst of clapping greeted this announcement. Willing hands from the audience helped to carry the grand piano down into the front of the stalls, and we continued our programme down there, making slight adjustments to allow for the fact that we could not use our more bulky magic machinery in such a restricted space.

It was fortunate for us that we had brought so many changes of programme to Africa with us, for we needed them all that night! The hail and tropical rain, starting at about half-past ten, continued incessantly till half an hour after midnight. Then it ceased as suddenly as it had begun, and I for one was very glad, for we had been performing without a break for four hours.

The silence after the crash and boom of the storm on the tin roof was startling. I took advantage of it to thank the audience for their indulgence, and to wish them a cheerful good morning!

I was not prepared for the scene that followed. Cheering began spontaneously, and lasted solidly for several minutes. Then someone started singing "For They Are Jolly Good Fellows", and the song went on and on through interminable verses as the audience filed out into the darkness to try to get home. Some of them had driven several hundred miles across the veldt to see us perform.

I have not often felt at a loss on the stage, but I could

not have replied to that generous mark of appreciation then if I had been promised a fortune to do it.

The place outside was deep in flood water and presented an amazing scene of chaos and destruction. The men of my company joined me in a torchlight search for our missing magic crates, while the girls went off to try to dry their stockings, for we had all got very wet about the feet and legs during the show.

Our cases were scattered far and wide. One of them had floated fully a hundred yards from the stage-door, and fetched up leaning drunkenly against a fence.

The rows of cars waiting outside the theatre for their owners had all been more or less flooded with water. Most of them would not start for some time, and a rather curious little cameo sticks in my mind in this connection.

At about one o'clock in the morning, returning to the theatre and trundling the last of our lost crates in front of me, I came round a corner and saw the long lines of cars, mostly with their lights going now and adding an eerie glamour to the scene, standing in irregular rows ; while, with his head deep in each car's bonnet there was the busy figure of its irate owner.

We had to open a fresh show in Durban, over a hundred and fifty miles away, that same evening at 8.30. The whole company worked like Trojans till 5 a.m., when the scattered "magic" had been collected and dried and packed, and everything was shipshape and ready for the train. Then we snatched a short sleep, travelled to Durban, and opened crack on the minute, to give one of the best shows during the whole of our tour.

Later we visited Bloemfontein, where I had rather an uncanny experience.

After the show I was told that a Zulu witch-doctor wished to see me. He was shown into my dressing-room, and he presented a most impressive appearance. He was clad principally in bones, some of which were certainly human, and gruesome little "charms", and though he must have been very old his eyes glittered as brightly as a snake's.

He seemed to have lost his voice, so I asked him what he wanted. Then he plunged off into a rigmarole about my having stolen his rainstorm! The old josser was apparently accusing *me* of having stolen *his* rainstorm, and complained he had lost great kudos because I had done so.

I pointed out to him that I hadn't wanted the wretched thing, and that he could have had it and welcome; but that only made him worse. He thought I was being flippant, and stared at me in a very nasty way. He said that the Government made it hard enough for him to get a living by banning baby-sacrifices and other pleasantries of that nature, which, he said, were essential to the programme of any well-conducted wizard. Now I had come into his preserves, and, not content with prostituting the ancient arts before irreverent onlookers, I had gone into the rain-making business in direct rivalry to himself.

I had let him in to my room because I am always ready to meet a brother magician, of whatever colour, class or creed. But as this one had only complaints to offer, I asked him to say what he wanted as briefly as possible and then get out.

He calmly suggested that I should pay him fifty pounds.

I am afraid I laughed at that. He began caressing a little necklace of human finger-bones he was wearing, and for the first time I felt something sinister emanate from the ugly old ancient. I stopped laughing and ordered him sharply to leave my room.

"I leave yo' room, Massa," he piped in his shrill old voice. "Oh, yes, I leave yo' room. You t'ink Kulati silly old nigger man. You learn, Massa—you learn!"

He flung something at me. It hit my chest and fluttered to the floor as lightly as a match-stick. I stooped and picked it up, and saw that it was one of the finger-bones from the necklace. For some inexplicable reason the silly little relic gave me quite a chill.

"Get out!" I said sharply.

The wizened old man gave me another snaky look and danced in a wild zig-zag to the door, chanting something in a beastly high monotone. At the door he turned.

"You die or I die in six months, Massa," he shrilled.

Then the door slammed to behind him.

Well, of course, I have had too many strange visitors to my dressing-room to think much of a crazy old man like that. Within a couple of days I had forgotten all about him.

Some three months later, however, after I had returned to England, I narrowly escaped death when a taxi knocked me down in Kensington and another taxi skidded to avoid it and passed within six inches of my head as I lay on the greasy road.

While I was being picked up I was still pretty dazed, and I suppose that accounts for a vivid vision I had for a moment of the old black witch-doctor bending over me there in the street and staring into my closed eyes.

A month later I was cycling in Herne Hill when a lorry touched the handlebar of my bicycle and sent me flying into the road. I sustained considerable bruising, and was narrowly missed by the lorry's huge wheels as it rumbled to a standstill ; and once again a memory or vision of the old Zulu flashed into my mind with painful clearness.

Six months almost to the day after that old and dirty reprobate had threatened me in my dressing-room in Bloemfontein I was swimming in a summery sea at Hythe when I was gripped by the most infernal cramp I have ever known.

My legs refused to move, and the pain paralysed me.
I slipped down through the green water, and it closed
softly over my head. A convulsive effort brought me to
the surface, but the pain it caused almost made me faint,
and I sank again at once. Sliding down to the depths I
suddenly recalled the witch-doctor; and seemed to see him
lying in a grass hut horribly contorted in an attitude which
I think only some gripping alkaloid poison could have
induced.

Rage against the old man swept through my body, and
prompted one more effort. I struck out violently, my head
broke the surface again, and at the same moment my feet
touched bottom. I had somehow struggled back into
shallow water.

I often wonder whether my visions were mere coin-
cidence caused by pain and a subconscious memory of the
old man's prophecy, or whether he really died within the
six months, perhaps uttering his death-chant, just as my
imagination pictured him, while I was fighting for life in
the water. For it is a recognized canon of the Black Arts
that a curse involving life and death always comes home to
roost within the specified time if it fails to take effect on
the intended victim.

After Bloemfontein we went on to East London and
Port Elizabeth. At the latter town I visited the world-famous
snake-park, and was fascinated with my first view of the
place.

The pythons' enclosure looked interesting, so I entered
it and picked up an eighteen-foot snake which had a rather
friendly face. I was not mistaken about its character; it
twined itself over my shoulder and round my neck in the
pleasantest manner imaginable.

There was quite a lot of excitement at my act, but it
was neither foolhardy nor brave. As I have explained

elsewhere, we have a legend in our family that a forerunner entered into a compact with the Devil; and one of the terms of the contract was that no Maskelyne should ever fear a serpent, or be harmed by one.

The legend is doubtless all moonshine, but it is a fact that none of us is afraid of snakes; and apparently no wild thing, unless blinded by pain or previous rage, will attack a person who obviously does not fear it.

Anyway, I found the pythons perfectly tractable—as much so as overgrown worms, though in the jungle no animal, not even the elephant, will dispute the way with them, and they are said to be able to batter a stone wall down with their heads, or to break the neck of a buffalo with their powerful coils.

Later, the native keeper, Johannes, came up to me, and I had to leave the pythons. I asked his permission to try my charms on the cobras, but this he would by no means permit, at which I was disappointed.

I am an actor; this sort of thing, had I been allowed to carry out my own programme, would have been marvellous publicity for me; and why should I pretend that I would have been averse to publicity?

We spent our Christmas Day that year on a train travelling between two shows. Plum pudding, mince pies, roast turkey, holly and crackers were all present and correct, most of the items having been sent out from England specially. We had a very jolly time, but the temperature was 97 degrees in the shade!

During our South African tour we covered over 20,000 miles, and enjoyed every moment of it. I was very much impressed by three things about the country; the wonderful bathing, the opportunities that the land presents for pushing youngsters with courage, and the wonderful hospitality and generosity of the people. I have happy memories of that tour, but it is far too hot out there to make stage-work at all pleasant.

Incidentally, we learned a trick while we were out there. Miss Cecil Home-Douglas, my wife's sister, who had been a member of our company, disappeared and never came back to the illusionist stage. This strange vanishing trick was worked by a little old magician well known in Grecian times under the stage-name of Eros!

I cannot leave this story of my South African tour without reference to an experience I had in Pietermaritzburg, which I shall always remember as the most curious thing that I have witnessed in a life spent inside the mysterious circle of professional magic.

A lady came to my hotel one morning and asked to see me. She was obviously in trouble, and explained that her granddaughter, a girl of seventeen or so, seemed to be haunted with a familiar spirit.

Often, when this girl was in the room, objects would fly off the mantelpiece or table and float down to the floor, no human hand touching them. My informant was precise upon this point that the objects floated, and that even breakable objects like a clock or glassware were never damaged in their falls.

At first the girl and her grandparents (her father and mother had died when she was fourteen) had looked on this phenomenon as something clever and amusing, though the girl could not apparently "turn on the power"; it came and went of its own accord in rooms where she was.

But a religious-minded friend had suggested that the child was possessed of devils, and this silly theory had so preyed on the minds of the three of them that the girl was rapidly becoming a nervous wreck, and her grandparents were almost ill with anxiety.

Could I lay the ghost?

Well, of course, I am not a professional ghost-master, though there seems a world-wide superstition that I am ! Still, the woman looked in wretched trouble, and I thought I had better go along and see what I could do.

I went straight to the house of my informant, and met her husband and grandchild there. The girl looked nervous and unhappy; but no ghostly phenomena exhibited themselves during my visit. My status was not explained to the granddaughter; I was simply introduced as a friend.

I stayed for about half an hour, and then rose to take my leave. The lady who had brought me accompanied me out on to the verandah, after I had said good-bye to the others, and apologized for troubling me.

"I had expected to see something happen," she said sorrowfully, "because Anna's haunting always takes place when she is nervous."

At the same time we both heard a low cry from the room we had just left. Without apology, I ran back and opened the door.

Looking in I saw something really uncanny. The big clock from the mantelpiece was floating in mid-air at some five feet from the floor; as I opened the door it glided swiftly yet smoothly downwards and settled on the rug before the fire.

It was still the right way up, and was still ticking gently, though it was a pendulum clock, and any shaking would have stopped it instantly.

In a moment I knew what was wrong. With a murmured excuse that I had forgotten my gloves, I did an elementary little trick and made the gloves "appear" on a side-table, whence I retrieved them, and, saying good-bye once more, returned to the verandah, where my hostess was still waiting.

"I think I have solved your mystery," I said happily.

P

"Don't worry any more about this devil-possession rubbish. Your grandchild is a poltergeist, my dear lady; it is a disease very well known to medical science, though it cannot be explained away. Give the girl a change of air and scene for six months, and I'll wager my reputation as a magician that the clocks will fly no more."

This poltergeist quality is a strange and rare disease caused by abnormal nervousness in adolescents. No one knows just how, but a poltergeist can cause articles to defy the laws of gravity, and float about in mid-air, eventually coming gently to the ground, just as I had seen the clock do. The power is not a voluntary one, and seldom lasts more than a few months.

Change of interests is the usual cure, and very seldom fails. It did not fail in the case of my Pietermaritzburg friends. I had a letter from the grandmother, shortly after my return to England, thanking me in far too extravagant language for that simple service which my knowledge of all things magic had enabled me to perform.

The girl had shown no more symptoms of the poltergeist state after they had got her a job in a distant town. She was now very happy, her health had come racing back, and there was a hint that she was more or less engaged. I was very delighted at her cure.

I still have that letter, together with the finger-bone which the Zulu wizard threw at me, and one or two other mementoes of my South African tour, in our Maskelyne magic museum. I hope the girl has found real happiness since; and nowadays I can even spare a good wish for the naughty old witch-doctor, though for the first six months after I met him I was inclined to curse him frequently and long.

May they cool his toes occasionally on my behalf in the place where he has gone!

CHAPTER XVIII

The ghosts from the plague-pit—My first Royal Command show on
my own—A children's garden party—I am dismissed from St.
George's Hall—Starting alone—Appearing before the Queen—
St. George's Hall shuts down—Adventures on tour—"Jasper,
the husband's fear".

MY reputation for laying ghosts seemed to have preceded
me back from South Africa. For one of the first things I
was asked to do after my return was to settle the hash of a
peculiarly troublesome spectre in a night-club.

You and I, of course, would have thought a ghost
most appropriate to such a place, and an added attraction
to revellers. But somehow this apparition seems to have
exceeded the code laid down in the best uncanny circles.

So troublesome did it become, indeed, that the
proprietors of the Moulin Rouge Club in Brixton called
in the police to try to arrest it. But I understand that it just
uttered a thin wail and vanished when invited to "Come
quiet and it'll be the better fer you !" The officers then took
down the wail and altered it and prepared to use it in
evidence against the apparition, if ever captured; and
left the world to darkness and to me.

Meanwhile some bright individual had discovered that
the Moulin Rouge Night Club had been built over what
had been a huge death-pit at the time of the Great Plague.
I am told that a famous clergyman was approached to see
if he would "cleanse" the place of its ghostly visitants, but
he very sensibly said that he thought temporal interference
could do more than spiritual in this case—and he was right.

Within a week or so after the first report of the haunting,

the newspapers were taking an interest, and the affair became a national concern. The ghosts, it seemed, used to moan and wail, and to cause lights to appear and disappear within the building after it was locked up for the night.

These lights had first attracted attention to the haunting when a passing policeman noticed gleams in the windows at about two o'clock in the morning.

On the night of May 12th, 1931, a group of newspaper representatives spent the night inside the Moulin Rouge Club. Every room was locked, every window bolted, and the keys of the place reposed in the room where the watchers sat waiting, in complete darkness. The main electric light switch of the building had been turned off.

At twenty minutes to three in the morning all the electric lights in the place suddenly switched on one by one, apparently of their own accord. I should mention that the main switch of the building was in a locked room with no window.

The building, which was already surrounded by waiting police, was enclosed in a cordon of blue and then thoroughly searched. Nothing and no one was found ; but about an hour later a glass sandwich-dish sailed in through one of the windows and smashed to atoms on the floor, missing the head of one of the pressmen by about six inches.

The interesting thing was that no one could imagine where the dish had come from, since the window in question was about seventy feet away from the nearest thoroughfare, and seventy feet is an amazing throw with a heavy glass dish, even when there are no watchful policemen about.

The next night I joined the *posse* of watchers inside the haunted building. At ten minutes to three, scratchings, clicks and unearthly cries were heard from two different sources. Lights began to appear and vanish, and the waiting investigators ran in the directions from which the sounds came.

Meanwhile I slipped from my place and hurried silently down into an alley which a previous search had made me suspect. There I found two girls in black dance-frocks and a man in a dark suit. The "ghosts" were a lot more startled than I was when I walked up to them.

A whistle brought an inspector of police on my heels. The whole affair proved to be a practical joke, the practical part of it being to attract business to the neighbourhood.

As I have said elsewhere, on more than one occasion, I am still waiting to meet what one might call a "real" ghost.

In May, 1932, I received a very happy surprise. I was asked to appear in a Royal Variety Performance before the late King George and Queen Mary, at the Palladium Theatre. It was my first proper Command Performance, and I looked forward to it with both exhilaration and nervousness.

A splendid company had been engaged, including such famous stars as Cicely Courtneidge, Jack Buchanan, Will Fyffe, G. S. Melvin, Vesta Victoria and Jack Hylton's Band.

My choice of illusions included four tricks in which the distinguished audience seemed especially interested. The first was one in which I put some water in a glass bowl, added a handful of sand, stirred the mixture into mud, and then put my hand in the bowl under the water and drew out two or three handfuls of perfectly dry, powdery sand.

I produced some eggs from nowhere, performed a musical bell trick, and finally gave a demonstration that fishermen friends of mine have often openly envied.

I came on to the stage carrying a fisherman's rod and

line and a glass bowl of goldfish. The line was as innocent
of fish as that of the veriest tyro ; but I cast in the direction
of the footlights and a few seconds later a goldfish was
suddenly seen, apparently having materialized out of thin
air, on my hook, while the bowl now contained one less
fish than before.

Another flip of the rod, and the fish had vanished from
the line and appeared again in the bowl. I may say that a
rubber fish is used in this illusion, since the mouth of a real
one would certainly get damaged.

But the rubber fish contains a delicate little apparatus
to make it wriggle and flop about on the hook and swim
round the bowl when it is returned there afterwards.
This apparatus caused me an embarrassing moment at the
Royal Performance.

It must have been wound up rather too strongly ;
anyway, there was a hectic second when I was standing
with my line cast, and the toy fish was flopping wildly
about in my sleeve, trying to emerge on to the stage and
make an independent bow to the audience !

Fortunately I was able to appear perfectly at ease (at
considerable strain to myself!), the fish appeared duly in
its place on the hook, and the trick was finished without
anyone but myself realizing how near I had been to a
catastrophe.

Only a week or two after this Command show I was
appearing before another Royal person—the Hon. Gerald
Lascelles, son of Princess Mary. The occasion was that of
a Children's Garden Party at Marlborough House, Queen
Alexandra's former residence in London.

The party was an enormous success. There was a switch-
back railway of magnificent proportions, a toboggan run,
roundabouts, houp-la ! a balloon-bursting contest which
attracted much noisy patronage, a complete circus, a

shooting-gallery, and wonderful arrangements for refreshments.

The whole affair was arranged in support of the Children's Hospital, Great Ormond Street, to which Sir James Barrie had formerly presented all rights of his play *Peter Pan*.

I enjoyed this garden-party very much indeed ; I always get great fun when performing before children.

Towards the end of January, 1933, an event occurred that formed a turning-point in my life. It did more than that ; it was, I believe, fairly largely responsible for the disappearance from the London theatre world of the name of Maskelyne, which had shone resplendent there from the time when my grandfather first stormed into the metropolis with his magic show.

It was nothing less than my own dismissal from St. George's Hall !

The story is not one to dwell upon, though I am certainly not ashamed of my own part in it. I will tell you briefly how it happened.

Alone of my generation of Maskelynes, I had taken up professional magic in my youth and worked before the public at St. George's Hall ever since. I was only twenty when I gave my first show there, with my father. He and I carried on together until his death ; and after that, for many years, right up to 1933, I was the controlling influence in the place.

I claim that I did pretty well. In face of tremendous rivalry from dozens of new and old theatres and hundreds of cinemas, I kept receipts up and managed to produce attractive shows.

But my brothers, one of whom was trained as a wireless engineer and the other as an expert on lifts, decided in 1933 that they knew more about public entertainment than I did, who had earned my keep at it all my adult life. I disagreed. I pointed out—perhaps rather too forcibly for a youngest brother—that magic was an art and a profession, not just a thing capable of being understood by a dilettante who spent a few hours a week looking over the theatre receipt books.

I am hot-tempered. Doubtless I said things which were not tactful or soothing. I blame myself bitterly now, because in this way I was at least partly responsible for the break-up of Maskelyne's Theatre.

Anyway, I lost the argument. I lost it so completely that I received my notice as well, and an indication with it that the sooner I quitted St. George's Hall the more pleasant the place would seem to those who were left.

It was, I don't mind admitting, something in the nature of a knock-out for me.

What was I to do ? I had no provincial tour fixed up— and these things have to be arranged months in advance as a rule. I had no manager. Worst of all, I had no apparatus ; and a magician these days without apparatus is about as well off as a printer without a press, or a soldier without a uniform or weapons.

Let it be confessed—I did not even have very much money available to buy it, and magic apparatus is very costly stuff, a single item occasionally costing two or three hundred pounds. I was married and had a couple of small children ; I had lived well, expecting that Maskelynes was an institution that would go on for ever.

In this situation—and it was truly a tragic and terrifying one for me—my wife was my good angel and my inspiration. Without her, I might have dropped out of the entertainment world altogether. She it was who inspired me to try, in face of all my difficulties, in spite of the stunning suddenness with which I found myself out of a job and unwanted, to build up a reputation on my own—to try to fit the giant mantle of J. N. on my own shoulders.

I will not bore you with the full details of my next moves. Suffice it to say that—because of my wife's faith in me—I spent on magic apparatus all the money we possessed, except half a crown for myself and enough to keep her and the children for a week. My last five pounds were expended on a return railway ticket to Glasgow, where I had obtained a week's engagement at the Empire.

For the week preceding my trip north I was running non-stop magic from three o'clock to eleven at St. George's Hall, sleeping from midnight to four in the morning, and working from four till three in the afternoon putting my magic apparatus together and testing it out.

Glasgow, with only half a crown between me and financial dissolution, looked very forbidding. And it certainly *was* very cold.

I found a lodging where they would take me in on the chance of my theatre engagement being successful.

I have had a very warm spot in my heart for Glasgow ever since that evening ! I was nervous and excited, and it seemed to me that I did not give the best performance of which I was capable ; but Glasgow took me to its heart.

Bless you, Glasgow ! You made a magician that night !

That was on February 13th ; and my week's engagement was so satisfactory that I received offers from other provincial theatres before it was half over. Still, things might have been difficult but for the fact that I was commanded to appear, on February 24th, before Queen Mary, at a special matinée in aid of Queen Mary's Hospital, the show to be staged at His Majesty's Theatre in London.

It is a fact that I have always remembered with pride that I was the only artiste who had appeared at the Command

Show the previous May whom the Queen included in the list for her Hospital matinée so soon afterwards.

This Royal Performance, of course, gave my bookings a tremendous fillip. I was wanted everywhere. In London I was very soon showing at the Palladium and elsewhere.

And Maskelynes' Theatre meanwhile ? Well, it just hit a patch of bad luck. I longed to offer my experience to help it through, but I knew it would not have been any good doing so.

A big Diamond Jubilee Performance was advertised, to celebrate the passing of sixty years since my grandfather first gave a magic show in London. It was a wonderful success, and magicians from all over the world attended, in addition to a fashionable audience.

Among the latter were numbers of grey-bearded men and elderly ladies who had first visited Maskelynes' Mysteries perhaps as long as half a century or more previously. Some of them remembered the first performances at St. George's Hall, and had followed the fortunes of Maskelyne and Cooke from the days when the illusionists first appeared at the Egyptian Hall.

A good many were personal friends of my grandfather and father. They little knew that the name of Maskelyne would vanish from London entertainment altogether within a few months.

I have heard since that then and at other times numbers of patrons whom I had come to know personally, during my eleven years' work at the theatre, asked after me, wanting to know when I should return to St. George's Hall. They were told that I would be coming back "in a few weeks" ; but of course I never returned.

At the Diamond Jubilee Performance, the Davenport Cabinet Trick was revived as being appropriate for the occasion. My brother Noel and sister Mary seated themselves inside the cabinet, which was just big enough to hold them, and both were roped up firmly hand and foot by a committee from the audience. Tambourines, bells, slates and pencils were placed in the cabinet, out of reach of the prisoners' manacled hands.

The cabinet doors were locked by the committee, but the bells and tambourines began to ring, and messages were written on the slates ; though when the cabinet was unlocked a moment later both prisoners were still tied as before, and the seals on the ropes were intact.

Several other clever illusions were performed, and the show received a wonderful reception from everyone present.

Towards the end of the same year, St. George's Hall was put up for sale, and the B.B.C. took it to use for their music-hall concerts. I have appeared there myself since, under their banner. What a pity that Grandfather's scheming and work should have ended like that !

My adventures "on the road" would fill a volume in themselves. I was lucky to find a first-class manager in Mr. Jack Whitmore, who has been my friend and adviser ever since. I found provincial and London theatre managers helpful and kind.

For the audiences I have met on my travels, from Cardiff to Hull, from Land's End to John o' Groats, no words are good enough ! I must just say—"Thank you !" and again—"Thank you!"

One trouble, however, caused me endless annoyance during the first months of my new adventures. It was this :

A magician's illusions are made to impress his audience in front of the footlights, with sometimes an indulgence towards a committee who come up and stand about on the stage. From behind the curtain, however, the whole bag of tricks is open to vulgar inspection.

In a good 50 per cent of our big illusions, stage-hands

have to assist out of sight in the wings or up in the flies. Consequently, our greatest secrets are no secrets to them.

When I first started touring, I overlooked this salient fact. I began to produce the very best tricks that I had staged at St. George's Hall, where all our assistants were as loyal as bulldogs, and many of them venerated the memory of my grandfather as well.

My new tricks caused a sensation in the theatres I visited. But alas for human nature! Other magicians, who desperately wanted to learn the secrets of those tricks, marched on my trail, standing drinks to good fellows among the stage-hands who had assisted me, offering a five-pound note here and some other inducement there, just for a couple of words of explanation—"to settle a bet"—about the way I did this or that.

And, of course, this and that began immediately afterwards to appear in other theatres, under the ægis of rival magicians.

So I learned to restrain my youthful enthusiasm to offer the public the very best tricks from my magic repertoire. There are one or two, from year to year, that I put aside to produce only when I have my own theatre again, when the problem of leaking secrets should not arise. Meanwhile, I do very well with what I have available outside this selection.

One of the most amusing things that my venturing outside the charmed circle of St. George's Hall caused to happen to me was the flood of anonymous letters I began to receive accusing me of using my magic powers for wicked purposes.

Candidly, after I had had a dozen or two of these letters, from places scattered up and down the country, I began to be quite afraid to go home alone on a dark night!

I was told that I really possessed occult powers; that

I used them for such things as "carrying out invisible robberies" (I quote from an old letter before me as I write); and that I was the head of a great international crime gang.

It is astounding what an amount of superstition still exists in this enlightened land !

The proprietor of a restaurant where I used to go frequently when I was in London one day showed me—with a pardonable grin, I must admit—a long screed *he* had just received about me. It warned him not to let me patronize his hotel any more, and explained that I came there for the purpose of hypnotizing clients, and bending them to serve my evil purposes when I wanted any special crimes committed in which I objected to appearing in person.

From what the writer said, I was no end of a "husband's fear"; a dashing mixture of Crippen and Sikes and Dr. Nikola and Roaring Rupe the Hold-up King !

These curious epistles have pursued me throughout my public life, ever since I left St. George's Hall. I can only assume that my detractors thought that so long as a magician kept within his own little circle he could not do much harm; but that he should not come outside it.

I might also mention that I have been seriously credited with the power of healing by the laying-on of hands. To those who believe this, I habitually reply that I have no such gifts—I only wish I had.

Once, at least, a lad was brought to me by his mother, at a theatre where I was appearing at Leicester. The poor woman not only sincerely believed that I could heal her boy of a slight stutter he had recently developed, but refused to accept my statement that I could not do so, and almost insisted that I should try, even though I did not think myself that it would do any good.

It was a dreadful position. Rather than refuse, I put my hands on the lad's shoulders, stared hard at him, and told

him that his stutter was only a temporary nervous trouble—
that he imagined that it would come, and that it did come.
Now he was to think terribly hard that it would never come
again.

"All right, sir, I will," he answered, without a trace of
hesitation or stutter !

And I have received two or three letters since—which
make me feel like a hypocrite—from the mother saying that
he has never stuttered since that day. Yet obviously I did
nothing more than suggest the idea to the boy ; I couldn't
hypnotize a sausage !

Indeed, I only wish I could cure myself of 'flu, from a
most degrading attack of which I am suffering even as I pen
these words.

CHAPTER XIX

SOME of my most amusing adventures as a magician have
taken place at private parties where I have appeared
professionally.

The atmosphere of such parties is conducive to my
art. The guests are gathered for the actual purpose of
enjoying themselves. They are friends who are all looking
forward to being entertained ; all they ask is a rattling good
show, without caring very much whether they can guess
the "works" or not.

Particularly at Christmas, when I am called upon to
amuse children's parties all over the country, do I feel that I
have chosen the right profession. There is something spontaneous and warm and delightful about children's applause
which more than makes up for other professional dis-
appointments and difficulties.

A children's Christmas party is my favourite audience.

I shall never forget one such party, which 1 attended
a year or two ago, at the home of one of England's most
famous sporting peers.

My host, who is a grandfather and, I believe, a great-
grandfather, is one of those lucky people who seem born
to be a pal of youngsters of both sexes. His twinkling eye,
comfortable figure and apparently bottomless pocket, from
which latter he produces "tips" more expeditiously even
than I can materialize articles on the stage, combine to give

him a great reputation among the dozens of boys and girls who can claim relationship or friendship with him.

At this Christmas Party of which I am writing the youthful audience was almost delirious with delight long before my part of the entertainment commenced. Having been with some difficulty quieted and arranged in chairs, they watched the curtain rise on my performance, and were thoroughly in the mood to enjoy whatever tricks I chose to show them.

I ran through my repertoire, and as always when the audience is a sympathetic and excited one, was inspired to perform my very best. I ended with a trick in which I borrowed a top-hat from the host, together with a huge pair of scissors, apparently cut the hat to bits, handed round the pieces to be examined by the screaming children, received them back again, shook them up in an empty cardboard box, showed the box to be empty, turned it upside-down, and then shook the borrowed "topper", perfect and undamaged, from its interior.

This concluding illusion was greeted with howls of delight, from which rose the persistent voice of a young lady of about five years old.

"You couldn't do that, Uncle, I'll bet! Could you, Uncle!"

But Uncle was not going to be challenged in this way in his own house and refuse the dare.

"I'll show you whether I can do it or not, my dear Cicely!" he responded with mock severity, and climbed up on to the stage beside me. "Would you mind lending me your hat, Mr. Maskelyne?" he asked.

I did so. He examined my "topper" a moment, reflectively picked up the scissors, and asked me if I minded him trying to repeat my own trick. I had no objection, though I rather doubted if he could do it.

Next moment, the scissors had sheared through the rim, and a large section fell to the floor !

Now I was standing within three feet of him at the time, and, since I knew what to look for in the trick, I expected to see something which did not happen. Instead, another and another sliver of hat was clipped away ; *really* clipped away from *my* hat !

I looked closer and closer, till the hat was cut into small strips, but even with my experience I could not detect the illusion.

Then my host put the strips into my cardboard box, shook them up, and turned to his audience, who waited breathless and silent. He turned the box upside down, just as I had done—but instead of the bits having vanished, they all poured out on to the floor !

It was comical to see the chagrin on his face. The audience rose to its feet, whooped, shouted with laughter and yelled unkind advice.

Then the amateur conjurer picked up the bits, and turned to me with a crestfallen air.

"I'm afraid I can't do it after all !" he said sadly.

And there was my top-hat in segments all over the carpet at our feet !

That was undoubtedly the most successful trick of the evening. It took five minutes to calm down the shrill-voiced boys and girls, who were triumphing delightedly over the failure to imitate my illusion, and wanting to know what "granddad" or "uncle" would do about Mr. Maskelyne's hat !

When I was leaving, my host took me aside.

"I knew you wouldn't mind my amusing them, even though it was rather at your expense as well as my own," he said, as he shook hands. "I took the liberty of palming your hat into the hall here—look ! It's no worse after all !"

Q

But the "topper" with which he presented me was a brand new one, and it bore, inside, the name of the most famous hatter in London. I need hardly say it fitted me perfectly.

I have met with a good many exciting and amusing little incidents at this type of private party.

Recently, when I was giving a show at a big party held in London by Lord Ellenborough, I arrived at the house to find that a splendidly fitted and lighted rostrum had been built specially for me. On the rostrum lay a beautiful old Persian carpet whose value would certainly have amounted to several hundred pounds.

It was an extraordinarily kind action to have put it there, but I must admit that I felt inclined to think about it while I was performing my illusions, terrified lest any accident in one of them might damage the priceless carpet.

Then I was asked to perform my sand trick—the same which I had given at the Royal Command Performance shortly before. In this trick, I throw some sand into a glass bowl of water, stir the contents into mud, and then put my hand in the mud and draw forth dry, crumbly sand which neither the water nor my wet hand has even moistened.

But no one can perform this trick without splashing a certain amount of mud about—that is beyond even my magic. And how could I possibly risk getting mud on this lovely carpet ?

I begged Lord Ellenborough to allow me to remove the carpet, but he laughingly told me not to bother. Luckily for my peace of mind, I had in my "bag of tricks" a mackintosh sheet. This I spread over the carpet, and then performed the trick perfectly satisfactorily.

At a performance I gave in Ipswich recently, at the country home of Lord Woodbridge, I met with a stranger difficulty still. I had to give an hour's show on the lawn, and showing magic in the open, away from friendly walls, curtains and so on, is always a hundred times more difficult than performing indoors.

A wooden stage was to be erected for me on the lawn, and I went down to oversee its building, so as to try to take advantage of any tricks which I could manage to incorporate in its construction.

Just before the performance was due to begin I was moving about the stage making my last-minute preparations when I noticed an uncanny thing.

A table on the other side of the stage was slowly rising into the air!

I strode over towards it, wondering whether I had accidentally run across a superhuman manifestation at long last. But it sank down into its original place as quietly and gravely as before.

I stared at it, tapped it and moved it about, but it remained just an ordinary uninspired wooden table. I scratched my head, gave up puzzling, and turned to see to something else.

Happening to leave it for a moment and go to the far side of the stage, I turned round sharply because I thought I heard a movement behind me—and there was the table slowly rising again.

This time, I cleared the distance between us in a single leap—and the secret was revealed, because the table promptly danced up and down and fell off the stage altogether!

A loose board explained the mystery. When I trod on one end, the other end rose and "levitated" the table. But it did it in such an uncanny manner that I must admit to a feeling of definite uneasiness for a moment or two.

What was more to the point, it was now too late to alter the fastening of the board. So I had to perform for an hour, with a clear memory in the background of my mind that

I must on no account tread on a certain portion of the stage lest the table vanished and exposed something secret in doing so.

Magic needs enormous concentration ; I was thankful to get my performance over—a whole hour without the help of stage properties—whout any mishap from the "levitating table".

A most curious thing happened when I was giving a performance at Grosvenor House a year or two ago.

It was at Christmas-time, and I was producing a ghost-raising illusion, in which the spectre of a girl appeared and conversed with me on the stage. Unfortunately one corner of the stage was not very well lighted at the time, owing to a wiring failure which happened on Christmas morning, when no electricians were available, and though using this corner made our illusion all the more effective, it was also rather dangerous, since one could easily step off the edge altogether.

As bad luck would have it, my usual assistant developed a bad attack of 'flu that evening, and I had to get a sub-stitute, who, though very good, was not accustomed to steering about in the less-lighted bit of that particular stage.

That evening, as the ghost and I were holding con-versation, my spectre did a more effective vanishing-trick than anything I have seen for years, by disappearing over the edge of the stage. Owing to the haze with which I surround my stage apparitions, and the imperfect lighting in that corner, no one saw her go.

She was a courageous ghost, for she lay silent where she had fallen, though she had suffered some bad bruises. I improvised a line or two to suit the occasion, and carried on with the trick.

That night, several people complimented me on the marvellous way my assistant had vanished. Most eager of those who praised me was a young man of title, who, when he heard the story of what had happened, begged to be introduced to the plucky girl.

That story had a curious sequel. Within a week the two were engaged to be married. When I offered my assistant my congratulations, she told me that she had known her fiancé two years before, when they both lived in Yorkshire.

She was the daughter of a poor but well-connected family in the East Riding; her wooer was the rich son of a manufacturer who had only recently gained a title. The parents on both sides frowned on the friendship between the boy and girl; squabbles began in both homes; and the girl ran away to London, where she got a job as my assistant, and earned her own living. No one knew where she had gone.

Some familiar note in her voice had echoed in the young man's memory when he heard my spectre talking to me on the stage. He had no idea where she had been for the past two years, but he made an excuse to see if this was the girl he had lost.

It was; and the story ended in wedding-bells—or should one say, that *began* the best part of the story?

Just before Christmas 1935 I was travelling to Derby, where I had an engagement for a private performance, when I became involved in an affair that for a short time seemed to me quite uncanny.

The train in which I was travelling was not a corridor one, and in my compartment was only one other traveller, a man who sat ensconced behind his newspaper so securely that I did not get a glimpse of his face for many miles. Then, having been showing very late the previous night, I fell asleep, and did not wake again till the train was drawing into a station.

I knew that we had not stopped anywhere since I fell

asleep ; when I woke we were still doing fifteen miles an hour or so—yet my companion had vanished. I have said that it was not a corridor train.

I looked under the seats, stared at the closed doors of the compartment past which the lines were slowly running—and began to believe I had been dreaming. Where could he have vanished to—or was he just a figment of my sleepy imagination ?

Before I was properly awake we had stopped at the station and a burly man in grey had jumped into my compartment.

"You haven't seen a man, five-foot eleven, slim build, black hair, horn-rimmed glasses, grey overcoat, scar on his left cheek, in the train ?" he rattled off.

What was I to say ? My vanishing fellow-traveller had been in the compartment before I reached it, and had hidden behind his paper all the time I was awake ; unless, as I was more than ready to suppose, I had only dreamed him ! I shook my head.

"Couldn't have joined the train after all then. Right you are, sir. Thanks very much !" snapped the detective and vanished.

The train presently drew out. When it was gathering speed, the opposite door of my compartment opened, and a man climbed into the carriage who had apparently been holding himself on to the footboard outside, out of sight. He was of slim build, fairly tall, and was wearing a grey overcoat whose turned-up collar half-hid a scarred cheek.

"You did me a good turn, Mr. Maskelyne," he grinned. "I vanished myself while you were asleep. Take me on as an assistant ?"

He seemed to expect no answer, but hid himself behind his paper. At Derby he slipped out of the train and was lost in the crowd.

Only once before in my career had I any experience of the criminal classes, and that, I think, is the strangest story of my whole collection.

I had just previously bought a very fast car, of which I was very proud, and I proposed to give myself a day off on Derby Day and run down to see the race.

I was roaring along the road to Epsom when I saw waving to me ahead a rather dirty little figure in a huge greatcoat and muffler and a green cloth cap. I pulled up, and was asked in a rather impudent Cockney voice for a lift.

Something about the cut of the little man amused me, and I told him to jump in. He knew something about cars, and praised the points of my new "steed". Under the circumstances, it was no more than natural that I should "let her out" a bit to show off her paces.

Unhappily for me, when we were thundering along at something over sixty miles an hour, a policeman jumped from a side-turning ahead of us, signalled me to stop, and pulled out his whistle. I was inclined to make a bolt for it, but discretion proved the better part of valour. The policeman, whom we had passed by the time we could pull up, came panting alongside.

"I'll 'ave to take your name and number, sir," he said, and triumphantly produced a note-book. "What speed was you doin'?"

"Oh—er—about forty," I replied.

"Thirty-eight, Sergeant!" interpolated my Cockey passenger.

But the "Sergeant" was not to be mollified. He moistened a blunt pencil-point and began stabbing his note-book to some purpose. He took down my name and address, the number of the car, the colour of my eyes and a few other details, and stared very suspiciously at me from time to time, as though to assure me that it was no use a-tryin' of any of my vanishing tricks on *him* ! Then he put his note-book in his breast-pocket.

He looked at my licence, leaned into the car to make sure that it carried no contraband, and finally wished me a sinister "Good morning !"

When we drew up at the Downs, my passenger got out and thanked me for the lift. Then he pushed two fat wallets into my hands, and disappeared.

One was the policeman's note-book and the other my own pocket-book full of pound-notes !

I can only assume that I was entertaining angels (or a pick-pocket) unawares !

I carefully removed that page of the note-book that bore incriminating details about myself and posted the remnant in the nearest letter-box. I wondered a good deal whether it was safe to tell this story here among my memoirs. But if the policeman in question, who I suppose could identify me should he ever read it, has not enough sense of humour to keep his knowledge to himself after this lapse of years—well, I can only pity him the reception he will get from his superiors, and probably also from his own associates, when he admits that he had his own note-book removed from him, as I had my pocket-wallet removed from me, in circumstances so extremely unflattering to a man of sense and perception, and, in his case, of Law also !

CHAPTER XX

I HAVE brought this chronicle of the history of Maskelynes
almost up to date. The tale of the great J. N. is told, and
my father's story with it, while the account of my own
adventures making magic up and down the world has
reached almost to this year of grace.

I think that the passage of time must add a romantic
colouring to the perspective of our lives ! Looking back-
ward, I can recall a hundred tales that I have had, perforce,
to leave untold, since this is one book, not a series of
volumes. Yet when I come to consider my life during the
last year or two nothing outstanding seems to have
occurred, and there is very little to tell you about it.

What have I done ? Let me see. Well, to begin with, I
have made some films, and I propose to make some more.
I am convinced that the realm of camera-magic has not yet
been properly explored. Indeed, I think that we shall see
some talkies, during the next year or so, that will provide
thrills even for the most blasé of cinema-goers.

These thrills will, I hope, be largely produced by screen
magic of my own devising, and in some cases of my own
acting as well.

For instance, I am probably going to make a series of
pictures dealing with the notorious Chinese wizard, Dr.
Fu Manchu. Most of the things that this mysterious old
Oriental was able to perform, with the invaluable assistance

of Mr. Sax Rohmer, I can already do in the studio. And I believe there are a few wrinkles, in the way of uncanny disappearances, decapitations, murders, abductions and sudden deaths, which I can offer the learned Doctor, and which, I fancy, will be quite new even to him.

Then I hope to assist in the stage production, in the immediate future, of a number of illusions which I have worked out, which are not only suitable for myself, but which might put some real pep into modern top-speed revues.

Some of these production ideas have already been tried out successfully. For instance, I perfected an illusion a short time ago in which a chorus of girls could dance behind a small screen in the middle of a stage, and immediately emerge on the far side of the screen clad in entirely different but just as elaborate costumes, when all the world could see that they had not had time even for the quickest of lightning changes of frock.

This particular illusion has been used in two or three talkies lately, and has screened quite effectively.

Just before Jack Hulbert started film work recently, he rang me up one morning, having heard of some of my magic tricks for revue, and arranged to lunch with me to talk them over. As a result, we have agreed to work together in staging a big revue-cum-illusion show in London, in which a whole series of my tricks of production-magic will be produced with proper effects.

In particular, I have what I believe to be an absolutely unique idea for staging a mystery play. In this play I propose to develop a theme to "vanish" the body of a murdered villain in such a way that no police force on earth could discover how or where it had gone.

As every criminologist knows, the problem that baffles murderers is not to commit the murder without being seen or leaving evidence—that is easy!—but to get rid of the body. I think I have settled that problem as far as magician-murderers are concerned, anyway!

Whether I should be arrested, if I staged this play, for giving tips to the criminal classes, I have no idea!

I have had, for some years—in fact, ever since leaving St. George's Hall—a plan in my mind for opening another Maskelynes' Theatre in London. I am certain that there are just as many people, and just as many children, who are interested in magic now as ever there were. Because magic is part of our human make-up—there is no one so sophisticated or so self-centred that he does not possess, somewhere deep down in his soul, a chord that will thrill to the eerie touch of superstition and wonderment.

For the past two or three years I have been gradually accumulating apparatus for my new venture. I have been perfecting tricks—among which is the Indian Rope Trick—too good to be risked in places where the more unscrupulous of my rival practitioners may possibly acquire their secrets.

Some day—perhaps some day quite soon—I hope to open a theatre in the West End that shall adequately carry on the traditions of Maskelyne and Cooke, and Maskelyne and Devant.

Against that day, I now spend every leisure moment in my workshop, whittling away at the machinery of new illusions, trying novel methods of staging our old tricks, reading ancient and modern books on magic, and gradually getting nearer and nearer to my dear ambition.

And learning—always steadily learning.

In one important particular, this plan of mine seems self-contradictory, even to me. For, if I open a new Maskelynes' Theatre in London, no one of my name will carry it on in the next generation.

My children are not to be conjurers.

I sometimes wonder if I am superstitious. If I had my life over again I would not choose to have one moment of it altered. I have had great triumphs, great happinesses—and great failures and sorrows, too. But, given a second chance, I would be a magician again—the same magician, getting sacked from the family theatre at the time when he was really obtaining a grip on fame, going out "on the road", meeting disaster and success, good luck and bad. *I* would be a magician—but I do not want my children to follow in the family tradition.

There is nothing wrong with the profession—indeed, I think it offers bigger chances now than it has ever done. But do you remember that old John Maskelyne, the Wiltshire farmer, whom legend says sold his soul and those of his descendants to a certain nasty little gentleman in black silk? It is because of him that I shall probably be the last Maskelyne magician.

According to this fairy-tale, which was told me first by my grandfather, sixteenth-century John arranged in his compact that magical powers should be possessed for ten generations, and no more, by his descendants, in return for John's own surrender to the powers of darkness.

Ten generations and no more!

I am the tenth generation. I am not superstitious myself, and I don't really give a fig for either my naughty ancestor or his grim little familiar. And yet—why fly in the face of the legend? . . .

I know one man who, I believe, will be sorry if the name of Maskelyne does not go on in the magic world. I met him the other day, to my very great delight, and he gave me a link, very much stronger than any legend, with Maskelyne magic in the past.

I was playing in Hull, a few weeks ago, at the Alexandra Theatre, when a Mr. William Morton sent in his name and asked to see me. I welcomed him into my dressing-room with a warmth that I could have found for very few other people in the theatrical world.

For Mr. Morton is ninety-eight years old now—that same William Morton who gave my grandfather his first real start in the provinces, long before London had ever heard of him. That same Mr. Morton, in fact, who financed young J. N. Maskelyne and his partner, little Cooke, when no one else in the world had faith in them ; who stuck to them and staged their turn until they stormed London itself and made a name in magic which shall not be forgotten— even though there are no more Maskelynes in the illusion business—for many a generation yet to come.

And what do you think Mr. Morton had brought me as a present ? Nothing less than that same original contract, signed by himself, my grandfather, grandmother, and Mr. Cooke, which made Mr. Morton the manager of the magic show, and guaranteed his backing till success came to it.

One of the things I am looking forward to really keenly in the future is sending Mr. Morton a telegram of congratulation on scoring his century.

I think I have mentioned already in this history that I foster a secret ambition to return one day to the old sprawling farm under the wood where John Maskelyne practised his wizardries—if he really did practise them— and take up the ploughing and the sowing and the harvest more or less where he left off. For what are ten generations to the ageless, patient Wiltshire fields ?

Well, perhaps I shall still do so. When I have achieved my ambition and rung up the curtain for the opening night of my own London theatre, and made it a huge success ; when I have engaged a talented company of illusionists and taught them how to produce all my best tricks there ; when I feel like amusing myself for a change instead of just amusing other people—then I shall turn my face to the west, and return to the land of dry-stone walls and grey stone-tiled roofs and red cattle and green fields.

I shall beat my levitation apparatus into ploughshares and—by a magical process, of course—change my stage-eggs into reaping-hooks. Instead of the applause of the gallery, I shall hear the piping of swallows under my eaves ; and, where now I cause rabbits to appear out of a hat, I shall then watch with joy the greater magic of my springing corn.

Then, when all is ready, the theatre carrying on steadily and successfully without my constant presence and the old farm-house swept and garnished ready to greet its new master, I shall perform the greatest disappearing trick of my career.

And then—as now—my audience will rub their eyes and stare at one another and say—"Upon my soul ! The fellow's vanished !"

THE END

INDEX

257

Lightning Source UK Ltd.
Milton Keynes UK
UKHW021259300120
357886UK00008B/1640

9 781290 181051